Finding
Fire

Finding
Fire

Cooking at its
most elemental

LENNOX HASTIE

hardie grant books

Contents

Vegetables

Baby cos, anchovies, smoked egg yolk	80
Peas, mint, jamon	82
Green beans, roasted almond cream	85
Calçots, romesco	86
Corn, kaffir lime butter, green chilli	89
Okra, roasted chilli, ginger and garlic	90
Beetroot, black sesame	93
Asparagus, mussel cream, rye	94
Broccoli, eggplant, fermented chilli brittle	97
Brussels sprouts, smoked ham hock, potatoes	98
Eggplant, shiitake, wild garlic	101
Butternut pumpkin, smoked ricotta, pepitas	102
Leaves, guanciale, pecans	104
Piperade, eggs	107
Potato, crème fraîche, bottarga	108
King brown mushrooms, raw beef, celeriac	111
Cauliflower, tallow, hazelnuts	112
Cucumbers, dill, horseradish	114
Pumpkin sour	115
Spaghetti squash, kataifi, pickled rose petals	117
Sweet corn brûlée	118

Seafood

Marron, finger lime, native herbs	122
Baby squid, pickled celery, ink sauce	124
Oysters, pickled kohlrabi, apple, sea lettuce	127
School prawns, chilli, saltbush	128
Pipis, garlic, karkalla	130
Red mullet, escabeche	133
Scallops, lemon curd, dulse	134
Sardines, bull's horn pepper	137
Prawns	138
Mussels éclade, fennel and saffron rouille	139
Blue swimmer crab, rye bread, lime crème fraîche	143
Caviar	144
Otoro tuna, fennel, edamame	147
Mackerel, bagnet vert, watermelon radish	148
Abalone, black bean, beach herbs	151
Flathead, kale, radishes	153
John Dory, cabbage, barilla	154
Octopus, radicchio, macadamia	157
Salt-crusted snapper, potatoes	158
Murray cod, Jerusalem artichokes, rainbow chard	161
Turbot	162
Eel	164

Meat

200+ day dry-aged beef rib	170
Duck hearts, celeriac, sour cherry	175
Beggar's chicken	176
Jurassic quail, toasted spelt, grapes	179
Bone marrow, sea urchin, purslane	181
Lamb rump, borlotti, nettle	182
Duck á la ficelle	184
Pork chop, sugarloaf cabbage, kombucha apple	187
Pork belly, roasted plum sauce	188
Goat	190

Fruit

Cherry tomato, stracciatella, black olive	196
Tomato rice	199

Mulberries, blueberries, smoked buttermilk ice cream	201
Pineapple, ginger and Thai basil sorbet	202
Banana ice cream, smoked chocolate, honeycomb	204
Blood orange upside-down cake	207
Peaches, almond cream, barley crisp	208
Cape gooseberry pavlova, elderflower cream	211
Coconut, chocolate, cherry granita	212
Rhubarb vanilla marshmallows	215
Quinces, mascarpone, pistachio	216

Pear and lemon thyme bellini	217
Lemon pisco sour	217
Grilled ginger daiquiri	218
Poblano caipirinha	218
Grilled peach iced tea	219
Chestnut roasted negroni	219

Dairy

Ember-baked cheese	222
Smoked ricotta	224
Smoked mascarpone	225
Smoked cream	225
Smoked butter	227

Wheat

Bread	232
Black bread	235
Flatbread, trout roe, crème fraîche	236

Bases

Chicken stock	240
Salt brine, 5%	240
Tomato water	240
Smoked water	241
Smoked oil	241
Fermented chilli paste	242
Smoked kombucha	242
Ginger syrup	243
Elderflower cordial	243
Salsa verde	244
Pil-pil sauce	244

KEY

Savoury
Sweet
Drink
Base

Recipes

Introduction

IN ONE WAY OR ANOTHER, I think we are all fascinated by fire. We're mesmerised by the flames that flicker as wood crackles and snaps. There's something about its colour and movement that comforts us to our core, and there's a sense of security around the ethereal heat and energy it radiates. Fire can also be unpredictable and powerfully destructive; perhaps it's this edge of danger that's attractive. Fire commands our attention, it stirs our emotions and, ever eternal, it continues its story long after we are gone.

Fire forges a connection between people, as we sit around it and share its warmth. It pulls us in and creates common ground – it's done this for millennia. Since man learned to harness fire for practical purposes, it's been a beacon for our rituals. Communal feasting around a fire is as old as history itself, and cooking over it requires all the instincts of the cook as well as a respectful interaction with the fire. In this way, the simplicity of cooking with fire is deceptive.

The modern kitchen has tamed fire, giving us ways to cook that are entirely dependable; but these ways of cooking mute the immediacy of the ember and flame, and the way they interact with an ingredient, slowly and surely transforming it right before our eyes. When we harness fire, we understand the full story of the ingredient: the unlocking of nutrients, the smoky transformation from raw to cooked, the way we need to read the ingredient and assess when it's ready to eat.

Cooking with fire is an extension of appreciating where our food comes from and a way to enhance our natural relationship with it. Like putting your hands in soil to harvest produce, using fire to cook is a way to rekindle our relationship with the natural cycles and, ultimately, with each other. It is elemental, it lays an ingredient bare; it makes cooking more intimate, more exciting and more enjoyable. It is also the hardest way to cook that I know. Fire's many variables defy a consistent approach and because of this, it never lets you take it for granted. With its ability to enhance natural flavours in ways that are unique, it is compelling, primal and an essential part of who we traditionally are. I have become addicted to fire and to rediscovering the grace of the ingredient through it. But the journey of finding fire has only just begun.

Finding fire

I was spellbound by this form of cooking. It was completely unique, so beautifully complex and yet so simple.

I SOMETIMES WISH I HAD A ROMANTIC BACKGROUND. I would love to tell people I was born into a traditional culture of food and fire. Truthfully, I was raised in the unpredictable climate of the UK, where the extent of my relationship with fire was helping to heat the house during winter and enjoying family barbecues during the warmer months. I can still remember the aromas created when my father grilled sausages: a combination of lighter fluid and rich, black char. The English barbecuing I experienced wasn't terribly sophisticated but I loved it anyway. Barbecuing represented the summer ritual of having family meals together in the garden, and that memory of human connection is far more significant than a perfect meal.

When I grew up in the UK, barbecuing was an occasional thing and often involved readily available ingredients. Although I always loved being around fire, I was a chef for many years before I discovered that it could represent the most beautiful form of cooking and be used everyday. Like many people, I regarded it as a fun but essentially primitive method of cooking that wasn't a feature of any contemporary professional kitchen. At least not any that I worked in. Fire cannot easily be controlled, so the only grills I cooked on were gas-fired, and the only real fire I saw was in a smokehouse. I couldn't see the fire for the smoke.

Like most young chefs, I was committed to continual learning and self-improvement. I chose to work alongside some of the best chefs in the best Michelin-starred restaurants. Each was an amazing experience and has shaped the chef I am today. But while I honed my skills, somewhere along the way I lost sight of the ingredient.

Modern food was moving in a direction I wasn't comfortable with; chefs were bending ingredients to their will, manipulating them to suit a dish and themselves, rather than accepting their raw and ever-changing nature and working with that. Such orchestration felt forced and soulless to me and I became disillusioned with the style of restaurant in which the chef, their technique and the look of the plated dish seemed more important than the ingredients themselves. I knew such establishments had their place, but I felt like I needed something else. I knew I had to put the tweezers down and make a change. I wanted to be cooking the kind of food I wanted to eat and, importantly, I wanted to turn to raw ingredients, not technique, for inspiration.

Fire became for me a kind of evolutionary throwback that made me feel alive again. When I rediscovered it, it was like taking a giant step back after years of running forward. I had just finished working in France and a friend of mine was driving to Mugaritz to begin an internship. Around that time (before Michelin went to Japan), I had heard that San Sebastián held the highest number of Michelin stars per square kilometre anywhere on earth. I wanted to see what made this Spanish seaside town so special, so I joined in the road trip. As we crossed the border into Basque country, it became instantly clear to me how distinct this region is and, as we were to be reminded at every turn, that this was *not* Spain.

San Sebastián's rich and affluent history stretches back to the late nineteenth century. It was where the wealthy spent their summers during the Belle Epoque. But it hasn't always been a playground. In 1939, Franco declared victory and became dictator of Spain. Basque political groups and expressions of culture were strictly prohibited and people could find themselves in danger if they spoke their native language in public. Despite forty years of political and cultural oppression, the Basques retained their identity. Upon emerging from the Franco regime, there was a tidal wave of Basque pride expressed through art, music, language and food.

San Sebastián, I came to realise, is one of the most beautiful places you can possibly find yourself; it offers some of the most incredible food and wine in the world.

My CV meant it wasn't hard for me to find a position in one of the three-starred kitchens. But, given where modern cooking was going, I found it hard working there. For me, cooking was always a lifestyle choice; if I wanted to continue in the industry I loved, I needed to find something that resonated with me.

Captivated by the Basque country, I stayed awhile and found myself helping out at a local *pintxos* bar. The food was simple, but it was honest. I cooked what I came across each day – whether it was the mushrooms I found in the local market or the fish delivered straight from the boats. Every day brought something different, although the challenge – to make a number of small, tasty items for the bar – remained the same. To me, this style of cooking felt real – instinctive even.

Victor Arguinzoniz and Lennox at Asador Etxebarri, September 2009

One night at the bar, I overheard mention of a grill restaurant in the Basque mountains. It sparked my curiosity, so the next day I set about finding it. All I had was the name of the village, Axpe, and the name of the restaurant, Etxebarri, which is hard to pronounce and even harder to spell.

I hired a car and drove into the hills between Bilbao and San Sebastián, not quite sure where I was going. I took many wrong turns along the way, but when I drove into that small village in the valley of Atxondo and smelled the wood smoke, I knew I had somehow arrived. The place felt like home in many respects, with its breathtaking backdrop of mountains wrapping itself around a small community. At the heart of it all stood the sandstone building that would change my life forever.

As I didn't speak Spanish or Basque, I came armed only with a letter of introduction, translated into colloquial Spanish by a Mexican friend. I knocked on the door.

The person who answered it was not what I expected. Most chefs are recognisable by their uniform: crisp, white and official. A tall man appeared in a bloodied white T-shirt, a pair of trousers and trainers. It was the spring of 2006 and that man, who was halfway through butchering a cow, was Victor, or Bittor, Arguinzoniz. He scanned my CV and screwed up his face. It was clear he wasn't interested in chefs from Michelin-starred restaurants and he made a point of saying so. Nevertheless he welcomed me in and, after showing me around, offered me a job. I would start the following day.

I drove back to San Sebastián to drop off the car. The following morning at dawn I set off back toward Axpe, though my limited understanding of the local rail system meant I was late for my first shift. The slow train meandered through every village along the way, so a journey that I calculated should take ninety minutes lasted more than three hours. I felt a rush of panic. I had always prided myself on being punctual; this was my first day at my new job and I knew that lunch service would soon begin. Still, Victor picked me up from the station and threw me straight to work on the grill.

That was it: my moment of revelation. I knew as soon as I arrived that this was cooking that would really move me. In a small lean-to off the main kitchen lay six stainless steel grills suspended over fire. Each grill was handmade and operated with a series of pulleys, cables and wheels; they moved up and down with ease. I had never seen anything like it. It was a magical instrument and Victor played it harmoniously, elevating his mastery of fire almost to an art form. Watching him was mesmerising.

Victor was so far removed from the trappings of a normal chef, more focused on the food and the fire than his appearance. He had studied to be an electrician, had worked in a local factory and then as a woodsman. He opened the restaurant in 1989, after restoring the ruin that lay at the centre of his village and calling it Etxebarri, aptly meaning new house.

Victor humbly welcomed me into his world, where I found a man absorbed by and silently conversing with fire.

Opening an *asador* (grill restaurant) brought community spirit to the village and gave Victor a livelihood; it was a place where he could unleash his passion for cooking and revisit the wood-fired flavours of his childhood. His lack of culinary training was very much to his benefit because although he respected tradition, he wasn't bound by it. His teachers were his years of exploring the subtle nuances of fire, and he tailored his self-taught techniques in ways that suited his unique cooking style.

Victor humbly welcomed me into his world, where I found a man absorbed by and silently conversing with fire. My arrival in the kitchen created something unique where our two worlds collided. In spite of having very different backgrounds and languages, a strong relationship based on a love of ingredients and a dedication to hard work sparked between us. While he wore a white T-shirt, I wore a black T-shirt. When my brother asked why, Victor's simple response was, 'Opposites attract'.

I was spellbound by this form of cooking. It was so completely novel, so beautifully complex and yet so simple. It highlighted the qualities of ingredients in their most natural state – unmasked and unhindered.

Victor and I cooked for ourselves and for the beauty of the ingredients. We pushed ourselves and the boundaries of wood-fired grilling, exploring different woods (something I still do today), removing the large old-style *asador* menu and opting for a more concise list based on the best ingredients available each day. We began grilling everything on the menu,

from cockles to caviar. Caviar took almost a year to perfect and was met with disbelief from the critics; how could we take such a fine ingredient and subject it to the primitive influence of the grill? We continued regardless.

We set about sourcing the right caviar for the grill. The ability of the embers to amplify natural flavours meant that the caviar had to be both unsalted and unpasteurised. We sampled dozens of varieties before settling on just one: Iranian beluga imperial ooo.

We then began the long process of working out how best to grill it. Trial and error led to the construction of a mesh pan that we kept adjusting until we got it just right. We devised a system of grilling on the mesh suspended over a bed of applewood embers, but the heat was too dry. It required another medium.

We had recently perfected a white asparagus dish that was grilled over a bed of damp moss, so we decided to apply the same principle, substituting the moss for a bed of fresh wakame. We grilled a small mound of caviar on the seaweed, over applewood, until it was warm and slightly smoky but still retained that characteristic 'pop' it gives when the eggs burst in your mouth. They released a rich sea flavour with nuances of black olives and hazelnuts. For me, it was a complete revelation.

We treated all the ingredients with a similar reverence, tailoring the wood and apparatus to each. Each time we tried something new, the grill rendered an ingredient in such a

Victor and I cooked for ourselves and for the beauty of the ingredients.

way that it was like trying it for the first time. Familiar raw materials suddenly took on a different life. They spoke a whole new language.

We even grilled foie gras, an ingredient I thought I knew from many years working in French restaurants. One afternoon we took a fattened liver from a freshly eviscerated goose; it was still warm and bright with life. Even for us, grilling delicate foie gras was new territory and we cooked the entire lobe over cherry wood, watching as the exterior slowly caramelised to a rich mahogany. I'll never forget the moment I placed that foie gras in my mouth, its outside firmness yielding to a rich, smoky, buttery interior. As I tasted it, I was forced to refocus and listen to the ingredient; it was as if I had never eaten foie gras before. Suddenly I realised the great power and potential of fire to enhance the natural flavours of food. It was a complete turning point for me.

At the time, Etxebarri was going in a direction contrary to what was happening in the food world. This was a busy period for Spanish chefs; they were the new cooking kings, espousing radical ideas that found ultimate expression in the molecular gastronomy movement. Both geographically and culinarily, we were a universe away from all of that. Our physical isolation in the Basque mountains meant there were no outside distractions so we were completely free to continue on our own path. Inevitably, our work became the focus of the

international media and Etxebarri was named in the World's 50 Best Restaurants. This culminated in being awarded a Michelin star.

I had completely lost my heart to fire and the Basque country. What began as a year in Spain soon turned into five. I had given up everything for this job, sacrificing relationships with friends and family to immerse myself in a restaurant. I had been completely assimilated into Basque life and had become Victor's right arm.

Etxebarri will always hold a special place for me but I reached the point where I had achieved all I could in that small restaurant in the mountains. The opportunity came to move to Australia and I decided it was time to pursue my next challenge, which is perhaps the greatest for any chef – opening a restaurant.

Firedoor

Our kitchen uses no gas
or electricity; we have two
wood-fired ovens, three grills
and a wood-burning hearth.

I FELT COMPELLED TO OPEN THE RESTAURANT as a means of expression, more for the ingredients and the fire than for myself. I hadn't cooked for four years and I didn't even have a menu – just a fire, some ingredients and a burning desire to showcase their beautiful relationship.

But there were many hurdles along the way. Opening and operating any restaurant in Sydney has its challenges, but my desire to use fire – and only fire – was hampered by planning restrictions, finding the right site and a lack of finance. I also had to overcome a general misunderstanding of what a grill restaurant is and, more importantly, what it can be. To this day, when I tell people that I have a wood-fired restaurant, they will invariably ask what type of pizzas I serve.

As it was, the length of time it took for me to open the restaurant was crucial, as the success of the restaurant relies on both the knowledge I have gained and the strong relationships I have developed.

When we built Firedoor, I had to design kitchen equipment around the demands of the space and our unique style of cooking. I couldn't just buy 'off the shelf'. Our kitchen uses no gas or electricity; we have two wood-fired ovens, three grills and a wood-burning hearth. All of the equipment was prototype, meaning the restaurant would be the testing ground.

The ovens were the first parts to be built, as they are the essential foundation of the kitchen and, in many senses, the 'home' of the fire. We operate two domed ovens that sit side

by side, dormant until the fire is ignited. We rotate how we use the ovens every day: one is for making embers and the other, with its residual heat, is for baking bread and slow roasting vegetables, fish and whole animals. When we cook, we have to time our preparations to be in complete harmony with the heat.

A fire is lit in one oven and slowly builds throughout the day, growing from a small bed of smouldering embers to a raging inferno. By the time the kitchen is at the height of service, the oven is literally a furnace, reaching temperatures up to 1600°C (2900°F), which is hot enough to fabricate glass. The high heat of the oven produces a chain reaction, igniting volatile gases that in turn produce intense embers.

We constantly feed the fire during service, replenishing it with different woods in accordance with what we are cooking, and how many people we are cooking for. We generally have about seven different woods on hand and every day select four or five, depending entirely on the ingredients we are using.

Our adjustable grills were designed to improve on the system that we used in Spain. We designed two pulleys instead of one, for strength and stability; a higher ratio drive system for quicker, more minute adjustments; and a completely removable grill frame, making it easier to clean. This ensures there is no build-up of unwanted flavours. Having separate grills allows us to cook the wide range of dishes we feature on the menu at the same time, and still retain the intrinsic character of each ingredient.

We compose the menu daily, based on the best produce available. This approach gives me ultimate freedom; if something isn't available or doesn't make the quality grade, it doesn't go on the menu. Our menu lists dishes according to their flavour profile – from those featuring light ingredients through to heavier ones – and this provides the diner with a progressive eating experience, which they can tailor any way they wish. We often have limited amounts of certain ingredients and these are verbally offered to customers at the table or incorporated into a tailored chef's menu.

We work with many farmers, producers and suppliers, and I challenge them to bring me the best and most interesting quality ingredients they have. I invite them to the restaurant so they can better understand what we do and I always emphasise the important role they play. I often ask them to bring me what they would choose to eat and I cook with that; every ingredient I choose has to be special in some way.

We kill shellfish to order, work with live fish, partner with farmers to grow bespoke vegetables, and age meat such as lamb, pork, chicken and beef. Everything we serve is touched by fire in some way – we even grill salad and smoke ice cream.

Firedoor is an unusual restaurant that is hard to categorise, but I'm fine with that. We don't offer fine dining and we are not entirely casual either, choosing to strike a balance somewhere between the two. We focus on quality ingredients grilled to order, combined with friendly, informative service. The space is open-plan, allowing guests a clear view of the

action that unfolds in the kitchen. It is my first open kitchen, and grilling would be easier without the distraction – but I've never taken the easy path. I wanted to invite people into my world and show them how simple it could be, and how good ingredients can become great ingredients when grilled over a wood fire.

I am proud of what my team and I have achieved, but, as most chefs know, the daily challenge never ends. I continue to work with fire because it pushes my limits, and that sparks creativity. The ever-changing variables of both fire and ingredients make this the hardest form of cuisine to execute, in terms of achieving consistent results. But every day the fire reminds me to listen to the ingredient. And the ingredient reminds me why I love what I do.

Fire in history
and culture

By putting one's hands in the
soil and exploring the natural
beauty in the food that fuels
our bodies – and by finding fire –
we are rekindling our most
important bond with nature
and thus each other.

THE STORY OF HUMANS HARNESSING FIRE stretches back over a million years. Yet today, most of us are probably more comfortable using a microwave than we are building a fire. For hundreds of thousands of years, fire provided our only means of cooking food, an ability wholly unique to humans. It is one that, as Richard Wrangham argues in his book *Catching Fire: How Cooking Made Us Human*, was probably the single greatest catalyst for our evolution. However, in an incredibly short period of time, our ability to use fire has been all but lost as modern methods completely supplanted it. Gas cooking has only been around for about 180 years, electricity for just a century. Cooking by induction is a recent innovation. So what happened to our relationship with fire? Progress is one thing, but it should never be at the expense of what makes us truly human.

For early humans, the ability to cook food was a game changer and fire was at the centre of it all. Our ancient forebears probably didn't realise that the cooking process unlocks nutrients, but I'm sure they appreciated the whole new world of complex flavours it unleashed. Cooking alters the physical structure of ingredients and helps enhance their salts, sugars and compounds. This changes the way things taste. Cooking forever modified the way we eat and digest; it reduced the need for incessant chewing because it partially breaks down food for us. It also allows us to quickly absorb more calories. This gave early humans more energy, freeing them to focus on other activities. Fire became the hub of a community and an essential source of warmth, safety and nourishment.

Cooking may have separated humans from every other being on earth, but along with that came rituals around fire and eating too. It brought us together. Fire helped establish societal roles, customs and cultural practices unique to the people of different places - fire, ingredients and cooking being the common ground.

By putting one's hands in the soil and exploring the natural beauty in the food that fuels our bodies - and by finding fire - we are rekindling our most important bond with nature and thus each other. The notion of the meal is a wonderful human institution - the interactions, the sharing and the problem-solving; there is much more going on than simply eating.

There aren't many cultures today that still rely on fire-cooking to survive and the proverbial hearth is no longer the heart of our homes. Yet fire still smoulders at the foundation of all civilisation because it has universally played a part in every single global community. I am fascinated by the role fire plays in different parts of the world. Although I may not cook with a strictly Chinese, Japanese or indeed Argentinian sensibility, I'm inspired by each of these varied traditions and apply the techniques of many cultures to my cooking.

When I grew up in the UK, using fire to cook didn't extend beyond the summer barbecue, but travel back in time and you discover a rich history of cooking with fire across the British Isles. The discovery of pit ovens dating back to the Bronze Age suggests a strong tradition of wood-fired baking. Hunter-gatherers would have originally used river clay to form a crust in which to bake fish, while meat was traditionally spit-roasted. In the UK, as in most of northern Europe, smoking with woods like alder and oak was a traditional means of preserving, so that certain ingredients would last year round.

Pockets of fire cooking do exist today, though. All along the Mediterranean and Adriatic coasts, meat and fish are cooked simply, over fire, with just some salt and maybe olive oil. In Spain, there's a strong grilling tradition that continues to be very regional in terms of the produce cooked and wood used. For example, in wine producing regions, grapevines are used as cooking fuel, whereas in Valencia orange wood is used

(see Tomato rice, page 111). In Basque country, which is more proudly traditional than other parts of Spain, the preferred wood is holm oak. Basques have a close attachment to their home, especially the traditional self-sufficient, family-run farm. Here, the notion of the communal table still exists, and fire remains central to the craft of cooking. Along the coast the Basques cook a lot of fish but no meat, while those living inland cook meat. This is as simple and as local as it can get. That's why we were considered a little different at Etxebarri, because we were serving fish and shellfish as well as meat in a mountain setting.

While Spain and other countries used distinctively flavoured woods, it was the Japanese who pioneered the fabrication of charcoal. Japan has an extensive history of charcoal making that dates back to the Jomon period, around 12,000 BC. The art of *binchotan* began 300 years ago, during the Edo period, when charcoal makers in the Kishu province of Japan used the local ubame oak to produce a charcoal of incredible purity. The same process continues today (see page 68). With its purity and efficiency, using *binchotan* is about as advanced as cookery over fire has become.

In Argentina and throughout much of South America, cooking over fire is a celebration for the community more than anything else. Here they like building a large hardwood-fuelled fire and they use it to gather around as well as for cooking. They don't let the fire touch the meat but rather spread the coals around the meat to create a source of radiant heat that cooks things slowly; whole animals are often splayed on a cross and cooked this way (see Goat, page 192).

Theirs is a big fire that brings families and communities together as a way to celebrate both their culture and the animal. They respect the animal by using all of it. They often put offal on the grill and use the offcuts to make sausages. The *parilla* (grill) can accommodate different heights, depending on the produce, and this helps control the heat.

In Brazil, and other nearby countries including Bolivia and Uruguay, the tradition is similar – but here the method of cooking is commonly referred to as *churrasco*. In Peru, food is cooked over charcoal, open flame, or by using stones heated over fire and then buried. This technique is known as *pachamanca*.

The many countries of Asia have deep traditions and a diverse range of techniques for cooking with fire, whether it be for street food or celebratory family banquets.

American barbecue focuses on the slow cooking of cheaper cuts, which also benefit from the application of smoke, spiced rubs and sauces. US barbecue at its most basic is the alchemy of wood, smoke and meat and cooking this way is very time consuming. You need to feed a small fire in an offset griller (smoker), which slowly feeds smoke through to flavour the

For hundreds of thousands of years, fire provided our only means of cooking food, an ability wholly unique to humans.

meat. You don't need much wood to create the smoke, and often another heat source is used to actually do the cooking. It is a very rich style of cooking, with a flavour profile to match; the flavour of the smoke matches the richness of the ingredient. This form of barbecue has become ubiquitous in America and is now serviced by a large number of barbecue smokehouses.

Then there is Australia; when I arrived, I had limited knowledge of how fire is used here. It was difficult moving to Australia after living in a part of Spain where culture and food are everything. And yet, by not being bound by tradition, Australia possesses a unique freedom and an opportunity to carve its own cuisine, based on a wealth of native ingredients and its rich melting pot of cultures. On arriving, I had to take some time out to consider the ingredients and the wood to see just what was possible.

I started by looking to the earliest beginnings of fire in this country. Stretching back some 60,000 years, Indigenous Australian communities carry unique and ancient wisdom. They have survived largely because they learnt to harness fire, using it to hunt and to shape the landscape around them.

There are communities that still live according to these ancient traditions. Take the Martu people, for example. They are the traditional owners of much of Central Western Australia and still practise old methods of catching and then

cooking their food, relying on fire to do so. Living this way is a part of who they are and is vital to their existence. Their traditional method of building a fire is incredible – carrying their fire with them wherever they go, keeping it in slow-burning banksia cones so they always have it at the ready.

We talk about Australia being a new country and in some respects it is; but in others, it is ancient. We would be foolish not to embrace how the people of this culture understand their land, its ingredients and the way to cook them. Nobody knows and appreciates Australia like the Indigenous community, who listen to its very heart beating and who use their treasured fire to its utmost potential.

Ingredients

Instead of starting with a recipe and finding an ingredient, start with an ingredient and find a recipe.

THERE ARE FEW THINGS MORE ENJOYABLE than
eating an ingredient in its prime. It can cause you to pause,
reflect and rejoice. Smelling the skin of a ripe mango when
its natural sugars have come to the surface. Pulling a carrot
up from the soil and marvelling at its vibrant colour
and unique form. Getting your hands in the soil, smelling
the earth, letting it dry on your skin and being awed by
nature's bounty, there before your eyes. The very tactile
nature of an ingredient, its aroma, its depth of flavour, its
aesthetic properties and the unique sounds it makes when
being cooked.

The fundamental roles of ingredients are to sate and nourish
our bodies, and to be savoured. But they have so much more
to offer. Science tries to analyse and understand ingredients,
which is great to a point, but it doesn't actually move me
emotionally. When we cook, are we cooking with our hearts
or our heads? I like to think it is a combination of the two,
because in some ways cooking is about striking a balance
between what you know and what you feel.

I believe there is an imbalance in most cookery. It is as if we
went down the same path with fire as we did with the very
ingredients themselves, and lost the connection with both.

I find it odd, too, that there isn't a greater appreciation of
nature. In the modern world, there is a lot of focus on the

appearance of food, but at the end of the day you are buying
an ingredient to consume it, not to look at it. You can indulge
in the visual aspects of the food on your plate as much as you
like, but the proof is in the eating.

In some sense, much of the modern culinary world's
techniques, expectations and food processing industries run
the risk of devaluing the ingredient. It is not to say the end
product is not enjoyable to eat, or something to behold, but
there is no connection for me personally.

It is much easier for chefs to demand three hundred uniform
radishes so they can control food costs and present precision
on the plate, but farming doesn't work like that. Produce isn't
so invariable. Food needn't be so manipulated. Nor should
craft promote wastage. Yet elements that are arguably the
tastiest are often rejected because they don't fit the ideal.
Every part of an animal or vegetable can be used, so why are
we throwing away roughly twenty per cent of what we buy?

We are the ones who should be more flexible and bend to the
nature of ingredients. Each carrot shouldn't look identical,
nor should every fish, and so on. If you take ten flathead fish
and cook them all the same way for the same amount of time,
they will not turn out the same. Their fat content and skin
thickness will be different, and they will be at different stages
of rigor. My wish is that each and every ingredient be left as it

should be, and cooked in a way that realises its highest potential. Their differences and uniqueness should be celebrated.

To that end, all cooking should start with the ingredient. Most of us are driven by recipes when we cook, so when what we need isn't in season we often substitute a dried, frozen or imported version, rather than create a meal with the fresh, seasonal produce that is available. We can easily get stuck in our ways and go to an old favourite as opposed to looking for the best ingredient, one that we may not have had experience cooking. Granted, it can be overwhelming.

The first step should be selectively sourcing ingredients in their prime. Instead of starting with a recipe and finding the ingredient, start with the ingredient and find a recipe. Buying inferior or expensive ingredients just because a recipe requires it seems backward. Besides, it is far more satisfying to buy, cook and eat what's in season.

You can look at an ingredient in much the same way as you look at fire; you can see when it is ready, when it is fading or when it is past its best. The ingredient tells us when it is at its best – and that is when you want it. All produce has a brief window when it is extraordinary. Some ingredients might be available all year round, but when you get them in peak season they are just exquisite.

An ingredient at its peak will have flavour or aroma, or both. There's also a denseness or weight to good produce, like it is relaxed and ready to be consumed. Think of the weight of a ripe orange, for instance. It is full of juice, and if you scratch its skin it releases a burst of citrus aroma.

Whatever the sign is for a great piece of produce, you can be sure that you will feel it has life in it. There is such a difference between carrots straight out of the ground and those that have been in your fridge for a week. It is the snap versus the bend. There is no point hand-selecting an ingredient by touch and smell if you put it in the crisper for a week before you cook it; you may have gone to the trouble of shopping and made decisions such as selecting one pepper over another, but after a week in the bottom of your fridge it doesn't make much difference. That fleeting moment, when the ingredient is at its prime, will be lost.

At Firedoor, I am never sure what fish is going to land or, in fact, what fish will be amazing that morning. Weather plays a cruel hand to farmers and fishermen alike. The availability of many ingredients, especially good ones, is determined as much by the elements as anything else. Farmers grow vegetables for months on end or raise animals for years just so we can be well fed. Our disconnect from the farm gate means we lack the respect at the final hurdle: where we cook and consume. I'm not suggesting consumerism is a big evil,

The recipes in this book are primarily about produce, about respecting it and about unlocking its true character.

but we should give a little more consideration to the source of our food. I continue to question everything I do, and so should you. You don't need to be an ethical or social warrior, but you should care about what you eat.

Selecting great produce starts with forming a relationship with the people from whom you source your food - your butcher, your greengrocer, your fishmonger, your farmer. In most cities and towns throughout Australia there are wonderful farmers' markets. They represent an enormous opportunity for those wanting to forge a better connection with produce, and to shorten the supply chain. More often than not the producers are there selling their fish, vegetables or meat, and it isn't long out of the ground or sea. This gives you a direct relationship to the source that no supermarket can offer.

Engage in conversation and don't be afraid to ask questions. There are so many steps and levels in the supply chain, the shorter you can make it and the more you can know about those stages, the better. You'll learn so much about taste, about freshness and about cooking. Then you can take your ingredients home and form your menu.

The more you understand and appreciate raw ingredients, the greater the connection you will have to them. There is a real beauty to this learning and this is why the recipes in this book are primarily about produce, about respecting it and about unlocking its true character. Indeed, the foundation of good wood-fired cooking relies on beautiful produce first and foremost, then the synergistic relationship between ingredient and fire, which creates an experience far greater than the sum of its parts. The biggest joy I have is connecting with and understanding the ingredient as it cooks.

Mastering
the basics

This is not old-school
barbecuing with flames that
singe your eyebrows. This is
the considered cookery of
wonderful ingredients.

AS AN APPRENTICE CHEF I never dreamt of one day owning my own restaurant. Working as hard as we did, I hardly dreamt at all. I kept my head down and pushed onwards, clear that wherever I was going, I had a hell of a lot to learn before I got there.

As with everything in life, reaching the next level requires a mastery of the basics. Once you have laid this solid foundation, it gives you the basis to grow – and a whole new world of cooking awaits you.

Sometimes it can be hard to be schooled. I remember one night in the restaurant when the wood was damp from the rain and the fire wasn't getting enough oxygen, so the resulting embers weren't reaching full combustion. This made it extremely hard to cook for a restaurant full of people, so I had to go back to basics and start again … building a small fire and working with it, gradually feeding it fuel and oxygen.

I am constantly learning new things about how different woods burn under different conditions at different times of the year. The best way to understand fire and sharpen your instincts is through experience.

Remember, this is not old-school barbecuing with flames that singe your eyebrows. This is the considered cookery of wonderful ingredients. It is more precise, more natural, much simpler and deeply satisfying. Embrace it and take your time.

CONSIDERING YOUR ENVIRONMENT

First examine where you are cooking – is it inside or outside? This may affect the flow of air through the fire. When setting up, keep in mind that all fire requires ventilation.

What are the weather conditions? Is it hot or cold, dry or humid? Cold or wet conditions may make it harder to light a fire. Is your fire subject to wind conditions? If so, you may need to shelter it.

What type of wood do you have? Know your wood and its burning properties as some woods burn at higher temperatures or a quicker rate (see page 69).

What is your fire set up? Are you using a firepit or a wood-fired oven? Make sure it suits your requirements and you understand how it works (see page 54).

The ideal environment for cooking over fire is an open area that is not too exposed. You are looking for dry conditions.

READING THE FIRE

Be aware of the sounds and visual signs of your fire. Learn to understand and recognise the six stages of fire (see page 45) while identifying the hottest and the coolest part of the fire. Listening to the fire gives you an indication of how vigorously it is burning. Smoke is associated with various stages of burning. The presence of flame and the colour of embers is a good indication of heat. Refer to the fire life cycle guide for further details (see page 43).

COOKING OVER FIRE

It takes time to develop a sixth sense for the subtle art of cooking over fire. In truth, one is never truly in control of a fire; you just need to work with it. There is no temperature gauge; the act of cooking is reduced to experience, patience and instinct. But experiencing that challenge is exhilarating, and the fruits of your labour will be rewarding.

Cooking over fire is about capturing a moment, enjoying the process of selecting an ingredient and then appreciating the way that ingredient cooks simply over natural heat. It is not just about the finished dish. It is every step you take along the way that makes the finished dish so special.

While there are many methods for using fire as a form of cooking, there are only two ways the heat can be applied: directly and indirectly. This determines how intimately the ingredient is in contact with the heat.

DIRECT Perhaps the most straightforward and recognisable method, applying direct heat sees the ingredient cooked directly over the embers, which may be intense and fast, or gentle and slow (see the fire life cycle graph and guide on pages 42–3). This technique applies to grilling and also to cooking directly on or among the embers or ashes.

INDIRECT Indirect methods work via conduction, radiation or convection. These can occur through physical mediums such as a cast-iron pan or a griddle placed on top of the fire. Salt baking (see Salt-crusted snapper, page 158) and clay baking (see Beggar's chicken, page 176) also fall into this category.

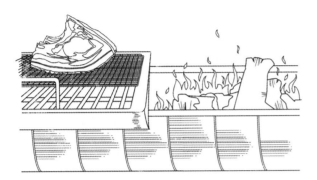

Indirect offset cooking

Two-zone (direct and indirect)

Food can also be placed adjacent to the heat source; I refer to this as indirect offset cooking. This form of cooking over fire is useful for long slow rendering of fats, as it avoids excessive fat dripping directly onto the coals and creating a flare up (see Pork chop, page 187).

Sometimes you may choose to combine both methods, cooking by direct means followed by indirect means or vice-versa. Equally, you may require both methods for cooking more than one ingredient at the same time. This can be achieved by establishing two zones. One zone is for burning wood, which can be used for indirect cooking. This also creates embers, which can then be moved to a second zone for direct or indirect cooking.

For your first time, gather some simple ingredients, light the fire, let it develop and wait for the flames to die down to burning embers. Hold the back of your hand 30 cm (12 in) above the heat source. How long can you hold your hand over the embers? (Refer to the fire life cycle heat feel guide on page 43.) You'll feel hotter spots and cooler areas within the embers. The intensity should give you an indication of when the embers are ready for cooking.

SHARPENING YOUR INSTINCTS

The fire tells you when it is ready for cooking and the ingredient tells you when it is cooked; you just need to listen and learn. It is visceral, not an academic exercise. Honing your senses will help you master cooking with fire. The more you do it, the more you will come to understand how ingredients respond to the heat.

Having learnt the six stages of the fire (see page 45) you must exercise patience. You can't rush a fire and you can't just walk away and expect it to look after itself.

You'll hear different sounds coming from the grill, whether it be marron flesh dancing and popping in its shell, fish skin crisping as the fat renders beneath it, the whistle of eggplant steaming on the inside - or just the burn of the fire. The first time I grilled abalone there were gentle cracking noises as it cooked over embers and I found it astoundingly beautiful. With time, interpreting these sounds becomes second nature.

It may sound odd, but when I cook with fire I feel at one with the ingredient. I'm consumed by fire and immersed in the moment. It is a profound connection that enables me to get the best out of the ingredient.

The fire tells you when it is ready for cooking and the ingredient tells you when it is cooked ... It is visceral, not an academic exercise.

TO CLEAN OR TO SEASON

I've always felt that equipment should be spotless before you start to cook. Not only does it enable you to cook with clarity, clean equipment elevates and retains the purity of the flavours of the ingredient you are cooking. Some people talk about grills being seasoned like a wok or a cast-iron pan, but if you are trying to cook lots of different things, any build up of cooking flavours can confuse things. A grill is not a bank of flavours. I once dined at a restaurant where a perfectly cooked kangaroo steak was marred by the flavour of salmon, which had been cooked on the same grill just moments earlier. Clean the grill once you have finished cooking and sometimes between ingredients.

KNOWING YOUR LIMITATIONS

Don't try to feed ten people on your first go. There's plenty of time to cook for groups and the recipes in this book will help you do that. But first you need to gain experience.

Like all good things in life, you only get out what you put in. If you put something on the grill you need to commit, stay there and see the moment through. You've chosen that moment in time, so honour it. Focus and cook. With such high heat, the moment could be over in a flash. Timers don't work when cooking over fire; you need to watch, listen, smell, feel and be brave. It will be worth it.

THE FIRE LIFE CYCLE

The ease of sparking ignition and the immediacy of those amber flames make it all seem fairly straightforward, but fire is quite complex. Put simply, fire is the chemical reaction known as combustion. It is essentially three components – heat, fuel and oxygen – combined in a chain reaction. All are required for fire to exist.

For a better understanding of the process, the burning of wood can be divided into six stages – ignition, smoke, flame, embers, ash and cinder (see page 45). The key is learning to understand, read and feel each stage of your fire.

THE FIRE LIFE CYCLE

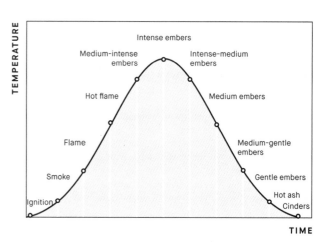

The following table details the fire life cycle, providing descriptions and approximate temperatures for each stage. To assess the heat feel, place the back of your hand 30 cm (12 in) above the highest point of the fire and count how long you can comfortably keep it there.

TEMPERATURE RISE	FIRE	DESCRIPTION	COLOUR	TEMPERATURE RANGE (depending on wood variety)	HEAT FEEL (30 cm/12 in above coals)
Temperature increasing	Smoke	Flaring wood, heavy smoke	Yellow flame, dark wood	100–200°C (210–390°F)	20–30 seconds
	Flame	High flame and smoke, volatile compounds are released	Amber	200–300°C (390–570°F)	10–20 seconds
	Hot flame	Medium flame and light smoking, volatile compounds are ignited	Orange	300–600°C (570–1110°F)	5–10 seconds
	Medium-intense embers	Low flame, exothermic reaction results in maximum heat production	White ash over glowing red embers	600–1200°C (1110–2190°F)	1–3 seconds
Maximum temperature	Intense embers	Hottest potential temperature point of combusted material is reached	Bright orange, almost white	1200–1600°C (2190–2910°F)	Less than 1 second
Temperature decreasing	Intense-medium embers	No flame, intense radiant heat	White ash over glowing red embers	1000–1400°C (1830–2550°F)	1–3 seconds
	Medium embers	No flame, medium heat, broken structure	Fine white ash over bright orange embers	800–1000°C (1470–1830°F)	3–5 seconds
	Medium-gentle embers	No flame, fragile embers	Grey white ash over ochre embers	600–800°C (1110–1470°F)	5–10 seconds
	Gentle embers	Decaying embers	Heavy white ash over softly burning embers	300–600°C (570–1110°F)	10–15 seconds
	Hot ash	Residual heat	Whitish grey ash	100–300°C (210–570°F)	More than 60 seconds
	Cinders	Cold remains	Uncombusted carbon	0–40°C (30–105°F)	n/a

Six stages
of fire

1 **IGNITION** Ignition is that first stage of lighting a fire, the spark that causes combustion.

It may seem absurd, but the temperature of the actual fuel affects your ability not only to light a fire but to maintain one, which is why heat is fundamental to fire production.

Every fire starts with the ignition, which can be caused by a match, friction, lightning or focused light. Keep your ignition as natural as possible. Don't use treated woods as they may taint ingredients or impart toxic chemicals. Be mindful of some commercial fire starters as they may rely on highly flammable fuel to help generate flames.

2 **SMOKE** The smoking stage occurs immediately after the wood is lit and heated, leading to evaporation of water and the release of carbon dioxide. The wood will produce white smoke until it heats sufficiently for full combustion.

3 **FLAME** Next is the actual fire, or flames. The fuel is burning away, flames are rising and things are heating up, creating volatile gases. There is a tipping point in this process when the heat is on the incline, known as a flashover. The released gases are ignited in an exothermic reaction producing an intense heat.

Make sure your fire is well stacked before this, as adding wood at this stage will reduce the temperature. In reality, many of the stages of wood combustion occur simultaneously; wood gases can be flaming and the edges of the wood can be glowing red as the embers burn, while water in the core of the piece is still evaporating.

You can cook with flames so long as they are indirect or offset; the flames should not be in direct contact with the ingredient.

During this phase, 'blue' smoke (in contrast to the billowing white smoke from the previous stage) is produced, which is ideal for smoking ingredients. You can suspend food above the fire for direct smoking (hot smoking) or siphon the smoke into a separate chamber for cold smoking.

As certain compounds of the wood are burnt off, the flames die down, the heat rises and embers emerge.

4 **EMBERS** Embers are glowing wood. By now the only remaining fuels in the wood are carbon and sugar chains of cellulose, hemicellulose and lignin.

When cooking directly, there should not be any fire from the embers themselves. Most people make the mistake of grilling over actual flames. However, it is the embers that provide the most intense, consistent and clean heat. Flames are still burning those volatile gases, which can potentially taint the food. When you cook over embers, the natural fats, oils and juices from ingredients dripping onto them can create a flame, but this should not be confused with a burning wood fire. This is the ideal time to cook.

Depending on the wood type, the embers tend to break down into even pieces and can be fragile, shattering like glass. The temperature of embers will eventually plateau. You can cook on the rise, but it is this plateau period that offers the most consistent heat and optimum time to cook.

It is fine to add more wood as you are cooking, but you need to be mindful that you will need time to let the flames subside, and allow the heat to rise again.

Once the embers have plateaued, the embers experience decay and their temperature begins to decline. This is an ideal point for cooking sides of fish where the majority of the cooking can be done over intense embers on the skin side and then turned to complete cooking the flesh side over a gentler heat.

The embers are now covered in a fine ash and almost appear dormant, but under the surface they remain a powerhouse of heat. It is not until you put your hand over them that you realise how much heat is still being generated.

5 **ASH** Ash is embers that have broken down completely. The whitish ash is made up of compounds of potassium and calcium, and has a beautiful residual warmth. A fine dusting provides an even heat ideal for slowly cooking ingredients like onions, potatoes and eggs.

6   **CINDERS** Extinguished combustible wood that ceases to burn, cinders are the cold remains of the fire. While cinders can't be cooked with, they can be used as a base for lighting your next fire.

Building a fire

You will be rewarded with the unique satisfaction that stems from creating fire not derived from the flicking of a switch.

THERE IS SOMETHING MAGICAL about building a fire. Gathering sticks and chopping wood takes time and attention. The primal act of lighting a fire is a satisfying ritual.

I was captivated as a child by my father building a bonfire. Touch-paper lit, the fire would magically spring to life with immense energy, the flames engulfing the wood and filling the air with sweet billowing smoke.

When building your own fire it is important to understand what you want to achieve. Think about how deeply you want to invest yourself in the world of fire. Do you want to dip your toe in the water and use it when friends come around, or cook most weekends and foster a real connection?

The Cirque du Soleil-like contraptions look amazing with animals hanging from chains or splayed on crosses. Though impressive, that veritable Ferris wheel of flesh is not realistic for the vast majority of us. Most people are not going to build a huge pit to hang whole sides of animals over a fire – nor use it enough to justify something so extravagant – but if you have the space and the appetite then, please, be my guest.

Everyday life is so frenetic that a complete switch to fire cooking is virtually impossible. But there is a variety of equipment available to consider, remembering that you should build a fire to suit not only the space, but also the manner and frequency of use. Fire is so versatile you can cook beside, under, over and within it.

FIREPIT

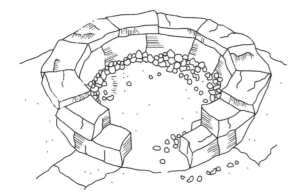

There are many ready-made firepits available to buy, and you can also make your own. This is something I feel you should consider as you can design it to suit your requirements.

While this may seem like a lot of work, you will be rewarded with the unique satisfaction that stems from creating fire not derived from flicking a switch. Trust me, the experience will change your grill game forever. A home-made firepit is also the most cost effective option.

However, a home-made firepit is a lot harder to move if weather causes a problem or you choose to relocate. You can buy a steel firepit that sits above ground (some people even use a metal wheelbarrow) and is movable. Steel firepits come in different shapes and sizes, but too small a pit will limit your activities.

If you have enough space, build or buy a pit that is wide enough to facilitate a two-zone fire (see page 41). This allows you to have a fire creating embers that can then be moved to another area of the pit for the purposes of cooking. You can then continue to feed the fire as needed.

A firepit is best lined with cinder blocks, stones or fire-rated bricks to retain heat and to enclose the burning area so that it doesn't spread out of control. You can also use the bricks to protect the fire from the wind and to create platforms to support your grill.

WOOD-FIRED OVEN

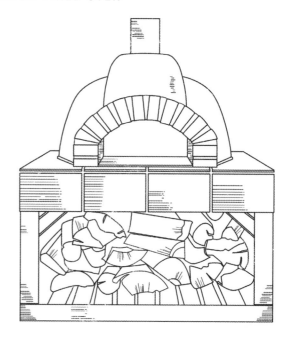

A descendant of the 'earth oven', the wood-fired oven has a rich history stretching over thousands of years in all parts of the world. Many civilisations have contributed to the design of the wood-fired oven, including the ancient Greeks, who constructed different types of ovens to produce different types of bread.

There are two main types of wood-fired oven, known as 'black' and 'white'. The most common are black ovens, in which food is cooked in the same chamber as the wood. These are often domed internally to efficiently absorb and evenly distribute the heat from the live fire inside the oven. White ovens heat wood in a separate combustion chamber and have lower ceilings. Insulation ensures that the oven retains a consistent heat.

While many people stick to pizzas, you can use a wood-fired oven for a variety of things, from smoking and slow cooking to roasting and the controlled creation of embers. These embers can then be transferred to the grill as required.

At Firedoor the wood-fired oven is where it all begins. The commercial nature of the restaurant meant that I had to design our ovens to withstand intense heat, which can reach up to 1600°C (2900°F). Most wood-fired ovens are not made to cope with such heat and you should be aware of this, particularly when using hardwoods, which burn at a higher temperature (see the wood varieties table, page 70).

Be mindful of your fuel, how much wood you are feeding the fire and the airflow. Closing an oven door or flue creates a low oxygen environment, which is great for producing good-quality embers. However, you are essentially suppressing the fire, whose only desire is to burn. Starving a fire of oxygen may result in a back draft as soon as the air is reintroduced, which can be frightening and dangerous. I once experienced an oven door that blew off and travelled two metres, reminding me that fire is a force of nature.

Whatever equipment you choose, ensure that the hardware is resilient enough to deal with the high temperatures. Don't let the fire get out of hand and never leave it unattended.

OIL DRUM

A recycled 44-gallon oil drum can be repurposed as a grill, as long as any toxic paint or residues are removed first. The adaptation sees the drum cut horizontally and supported in a stand.

Lining your oil drum with fire-rated brick will also help to insulate the thin galvanised steel. An unlined steel drum, which will lose heat and be unlikely to withstand the intense heat of a hardwood fire, is better suited to charcoal.

GRILL

The grill is incredibly important and something you need to consider carefully. A grill suspends ingredients over the embers (remember, you want to cook over embers, not flames). Having the ability to move the grill up, down or sideways, away from direct heat, will give you greater control when cooking.

Grills come in a range of materials, to suit different methods. Cast iron is fine but conducts a considerable amount of heat, which can result in heavy bar marking. At Firedoor we choose stainless steel as it is lighter, making it easier to adjust, and the bars are round instead of flat to minimise heat transference.

Before I worked in Spain my understanding of grilling was all about bar marks and an ingredient being charred into submission. But you should be able to cook an ingredient before that happens. Nothing annoys me more now than when the bars get too hot and you get those black, acrid lines. Remember, it is about the flavour of the ingredient. You can get a wonderful caramelisation without the char.

GRILL RACKS

Grill racks come in all shapes and sizes. Throughout this book, I use two main types:
- an enclosed grill rack with a handle (illustrated above)
- a grill cooling rack (commonly used in baking).

Enclosed grill racks are most useful because ingredients are supported and suspended over the embers and handled easily. Grill cooling racks are ideal for grilling smaller items directly on the embers. I also use grills (page 55), which are good for larger ingredients.

GRIDDLE

A griddle is essentially a flat piece of cast iron or heavy stone that can be used directly over a fire, negating the need to wait for the fire to burn down to embers. A curved version is known as a *tava* or *saj*, and is traditionally used in Middle Eastern countries to bake flatbread on the domed side. It can also be turned and used as a wood-fired wok.

INFIERNILLO

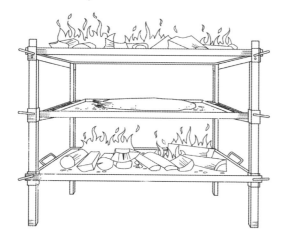

Infiernillo (which translates as small inferno) originated in South America and takes the traditional griddle to the next level. It has a second fire above the ingredient, creating a fire sandwich with an intense, even heat. Francis Mallmann is a strong proponent of the infiernillo, which he adapts readily to his style of Argentinian fire cooking.

CAST-IRON PANS

Cast-iron pans are very versatile and virtually indestructible, so they can be transferred from the open fire to the wood-fired oven to the table with ease. Cast iron conducts an intense evenly distributed heat, which is retained so that cooking continues in the pan even after it has been removed from the heat source. These pans impart a rich flavour and a natural iron supplement.

DUTCH OVEN

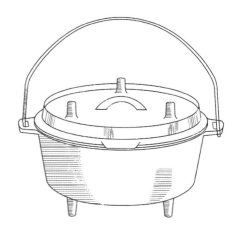

A Dutch oven is an amazing piece of cast-iron equipment. Portable and built to last, it is often handed down from generation to generation. By using dry sand to make their cast-iron moulds, the Dutch were able to produce a thick cast-iron pot with a smooth surface. The inside acts as an efficient oven, thanks to legs that sit the pot above the fire and a rimmed lid that holds coals. As well as being excellent for baking cakes (see Blood orange upside-down cake, page 207), a Dutch oven can be used for long, slow cooking in the fire.

PAELLA

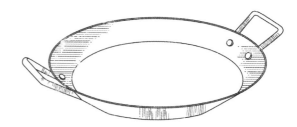

Paella refers to the wide, shallow pan used to make the famous rice dish of Valencia (see Tomato rice, page 199), in which it is also served. To produce a crispy base, or *soccarat*, it is important that the rice is not stirred, so the flat, wide base of the paella is designed to cook the rice evenly.

BUILDING A FIRE

　　　　BUILDING A FIRE

ASADO CROSS

An asado cross is a steel support structure for large cuts of meat and whole animals. The meat is splayed on an iron cross and hung vertically next to an open fire. The fire can be moved closer or further away to control the intensity of heat, while the cross can be leaned towards or away from the embers (see Goat, page 190).

CLAY

Clay is an amazing medium to cook in, providing a mediation of the relationship between food and fire and distributing an even heat. Partially porous, clay enables the ingredients to take on the flavour of the embers while ensuring they are protected from the intense heat. While it can be fabricated into claypots such as a tajine, many ingredients can also be wrapped and baked in clay, including chicken (see Beggar's chicken, page 176), fish and vegetables.

BRAND

The intense heat that results when you apply a hot iron to food, called branding, effectively creates an overhead grill scenario that's particularly useful for caramelising sugar or melting cheese, such as raclette. In Spain we used to scorch fresh sheep's milk with a hot iron to give the dessert *cuajada* its distinctive burnt flavour profile.

FINE-MESH SIEVE

Fine-mesh sieves are used in the same way as frying pans to sauté small or delicate items, either above or directly in contact with the burning embers.

FIRE POKER

This helps control the fire. You can break down the burning logs and help distribute the embers to allow for more even and controlled cooking - away from the actual flame.

FIRE SHOVEL

Together with the poker, a fire shovel is indispensable in facilitating the movement of embers.

METAL RAKE

A rake is essential for moving embers both in a wood-fired oven and a firepit. It will get very hot, so you want to be sure that the handle is not made of wood.

TONGS

It is handy to have a range of tongs. While sturdy tongs can help you manage larger produce, finer, smaller tongs are good for handling vegetables and fish.

SPRAY BOTTLE

Spray bottles are indispensable as they allow you to add a fine mist of liquid to ingredients on the grill.

AXE AND BLOCK

A heavy-based axe or hatchet is necessary for splitting wood.

GLOVES

Always keep heavy-duty heatproof gloves handy in case you need to move a grill or handle hot implements.

SKEWERS

Skewers are often specific to certain cuisines. They vary in length and are available in wood or metal. They make smaller items (see Duck hearts, page 175) easier to handle, and provide support for and suspend ingredients directly over the embers (see Eel, page 164). Those fabricated from metal also help to transmit heat evenly.

Lighting a fire

Whatever apparatus you chose, the fundamental steps of building a fire are the same. Fuel, heat and oxygen are the three elements required to start a fire. People often struggle when building a fire because they don't appreciate that oxygen and heat are as important as the fuel. It is often seen as a triangle, because without one the others fail to produce fire.

There are many ways of lighting a fire depending on your circumstances and the materials at hand. I prefer the 'log cabin' method, which promotes significant airflow. Unlike other designs, the structure does not collapse, enabling you to use it for indirect cooking straight away.

1. Create a stable foundation. Place 2 logs parallel to each other, approximately 30 cm (12 in) apart.

2. Bridge 2 logs across the first pair of logs; these should also be 30 cm (12 in) apart. These provide support for your fire and help protect it from wind.

3. Lay 4 pieces of kindling across the second pair of logs, creating a hollow.

4. Nestle your tinder in the hollow of the kindling.

5. Bridge 4 additional pieces of kindling across the second pair of logs, enclosing the tinder.

6. Bridge 2 more logs across the second pair of logs on either side of the kindling.

7. Nestle tinder on top of the second layer of kindling.

8. Bridge the last 2 logs across the third pair of logs, maintaining an open structure.

9. Ignite the layers of tinder at each level to create initial flames, which will catch and set the 'cabin' alight. Gently blow air on the flames to aid combustion.

WHAT YOU NEED

8 pieces of dry seasoned split hardwood

8 pieces of dry kindling made of split softwood, such as pine

1 handful dry tinder, such as pine needles, dried grass, fine twigs, shaved strips of softwood

ignition, such as matches, lighter, or flint and steel

NOTES

Always begin by making a smaller fire, which can then grow, as opposed to trying to start with a large one.

Ensure that you leave gaps for the air to flow through, remembering that oxygen is crucial to the fire.

Wood

Wood is a beautiful thing;
its rings mark the living years
and encapsulate the passage
of time.

THERE IS A CERTAIN SATISFACTION that comes from chopping your own wood. There's a delight in the journey as much as the destination, resulting in a real sense of getting back to basics. You feel the raw physicality of human exertion – the primal splitting of the logs with an axe – from the cracking sound as the log splits in two to the reverberations that flow through your body.

Each swing of the axe reveals a new part of the tree, divulging a little more information about the tree's life. Wood is a beautiful thing; its rings mark the living years and encapsulate the passage of time. The rings on a cut tree speak of more than just their age, narrating the history of the tree, the environment around it and how fast it has grown.

All wood is not created equal. In the spring trees grow fast, producing wider and lighter rings. During summer the growth slows, resulting in a darker, denser appearance. Look closely and you can piece together a tree's entire history: scarring deep within the tree denotes fire damage; narrow rings indicate trauma, such as dry conditions or insect infestation. A healthy tree has broad, evenly spaced rings.

THE NATURE OF WOOD

Wood is a beautiful raw ingredient, composed mainly of cellulose and hemicellulose (large molecules made of carbohydrates and sugars) and bound by lignin, which gives wood its strength.

Woods can be broadly categorised into hardwoods (such as oak) and softwoods (such as pine). They are classified by the structure of their seeds. In spite of their name, hardwoods and softwoods are not determined purely by density; some softwoods (such as yew) are actually harder than some hardwoods (such as balsa). The two types contain different ratios of cellulose, hemicellulose, lignins, oil, resin, turpines and fatty acids. Each of these gives rise to a different aroma that is notable upon burning.

SOFTWOODS Softwoods such as pines, spruce and fir are examples of gymnosperms, which produce seeds without covering. In general, softwoods are evergreen conifers. The lower density and highly flammable resins mean that they burn easily and quickly. If the resins in softwood burn they exude an acrid smoke, produce a bitter flavour and destroy the natural flavour of food. While they are ideal for lighting a fire, they are not usually recommended for cooking. Some varieties (such as cedar or juniper) are first soaked so they can be used for light smoking, whereupon they release their essential oils. Another example is the use of pine needles in Mussels eclade (see page 139), where the mussels are protected and subject to a rapid surge of heat.

HARDWOODS Hardwoods such as oak, cherry and gum are all angiosperms, which means their seeds are enclosed in husks. Most hardwoods are deciduous: perennial plants that are normally leafless at some time during the year. There are some exceptions, including eucalypts, holm oak and evergreen magnolias. Hardwoods tend to be slower growing and, as a result, denser, burning slowly with an intense heat. They invariably burn at a higher temperature and sustain a longer plateau once there.

Australia abounds in native woods, such as ironbark, red gum, jarrah and gidgee, which are much harder than those in most countries. Australia's unique climate creates dense wood that grows slowly and, due to the high level of oils and gums, burns with an intense heat. This explains the mass devastation created during bushfires that leave the Australian landscape scorched. Fire is an essential part of the plant life cycle, particularly for eucalypts, which depend on fire for regeneration. When I began experimenting with woods in Australia, I could not believe how hard they were and how hot they could burn. At 1600°C (2900°F), ironbark burns 750°C (1600°F) hotter than the holm oak we were using in Europe. It is quite extraordinary and, as a result, we had to redesign the wood oven at Firedoor so it could withstand the heat.

There are a host of hardwoods around the world that suit different types of ingredients and applications. The impressive burning qualities of ironbark make it a solid all-rounder. It produces an intense slow-burning base to which lighter, more perfumed woods can be added.

Most fruit woods emanate a beautiful balance of sweet smokiness that works well with a range of ingredients. Lighter woods, such as olive and almond, impart subtle nuances ideally suited to delicate fish and vegetables. Citrus is ideal for oily fish and the sweet brininess of shellfish. Dense mallee roots lend an earthy characteristic to your cooking, while gnarly grape vines release a rich aroma suited to red meat.

But remember, it is not an exact science. Part of the adventure lies in trying different woods with different ingredients and relying on your instinct to let the produce sing. It is as much about the flavours imparted as the heat given off. So don't panic about having the exact wood to suit certain ingredients.

SEASONED WOOD

You can tell the difference between young and old wood. Fresh or 'green' wood is still supple and full of vitality. Dry, seasoned wood is notably lighter, its colour paler. It doesn't have the resilient density of unseasoned wood. The sound of splitting seasoned wood – the way it cracks – is unique. Think about the way branches crack underfoot. A wood that is seasoned and dry can split readily (even a very hard wood, such as ironbark). If you struggle to cut something and need a saw, it is not ready.

Dry wood is also known as 'seasoned wood' because the wood has dried naturally over many seasons, allowing it to lose moisture. The maturation process of open-air seasoning has the advantage of leaching undesirable chemical components and bitter tannins, mellowing the wood as it dries.

Ageing, or seasoning, can vary from wood to wood but it generally takes at least two years (three for ironbark and oak). Lighter hardwoods, such as grapevines and applewood, may take less time, but that can depend on the conditions. Weather and the environment can play a role in the seasoning of wood; humid or damp conditions may lengthen the process. Freshly cut hardwood has a lot of water in it – up to 50 per cent of its weight. It is harder to light and emits steam and smoke instead of heat, thus producing unwanted flavours.

A seasoned hardwood will still retain 5 per cent water. Of the remaining 95 per cent roughly 40 per cent is cellulose, 40 per cent is hemicellulose, 19 per cent is lignin and 1 per cent is minerals, but the percentages vary depending on the wood species, subspecies, age, soil and climate. Although there are only trace amounts, these minerals can significantly impact the aroma and smoke flavour.

Correct seasoning results in a raised level of lactones transforming the flavour of wood. White American oak, for instance, is fast growing and produces up to four times the amount of lactones found in the slower growing French oak. There appears to be a direct relationship between the growth rate of wood and its subsequent flavour. The flavour will also vary with how the wood is dried and how long it is left to season prior to burning. The climate and the soil in which the tree is grown can also have an impact. Furthermore, the amount of bark can significantly influence flavour.

It pays to know how your wood has been seasoned. Some woods are sold treated or sprayed with a turpentine base to help them dry and age faster – and ignite more quickly, too. Some are even kiln dried to speed up the process. It is very different to have something that's forced rather than matured naturally and allowed to dry. Most things worthwhile take time. You are going back to the most natural form of cooking so why would you muddy the water? Just remember to care as much about the wood you choose as you do the ingredients. The reward will be in the eating.

COOKING OVER A WOOD FIRE

Wood contains a mass of phenolic compounds that are broken down and released upon heating. Sugar molecules in the wood caramelise in the intense heat and exude a sweet, fruity perfume, while other natural components produce the distinctive aromatic taste and enticing smokiness of the grill. The production and the variety of these aromas depend largely on the wood, which carries its own identity.

Cooking over a wood fire is the ultimate flavour enhancer, with each wood imparting its own unique personality to the food. The wood is as much a seasoning as it is a fuel, and should be considered as much an ingredient as the ingredients themselves.

Anything that influences the food that you are cooking should be considered in the same light. Salt, smoke, heat – all of it contributes to the experience on your palate.

Processed wood chips are used as a convenient means of imparting intense woody and smoky aromas to food, but they tend to give a one-dimensional profile that lacks the complexity of flavour derived from a real wood fire.

COOKING OVER CHARCOAL

Cooking over charcoal is different from cooking over wood, though they essentially have the same origin. Charcoal is manufactured through the slow burning of wood in the absence of oxygen to produce carbon, which doesn't have any distinct flavour profile. There are several different types, determined by the wood and the process used.

Hardwood lump charcoal is made from solid branches of wood and, like wood, will burn hotter at the beginning and cooler at the end of the cooking process. But all charcoal is essentially refined, closer to elemental carbon, whereas wood retains a complex array of other characteristics.

I would advise you to stay clear of charcoal briquettes as they are a combination of charcoal bound by other ingredients such as starch and sawdust. While briquettes burn uniformly, they break down easily to ashes and don't produce intensely hot embers. They may also contain sodium nitrate or petroleum, which will taint your food with a chemical flavour.

An alternative is coconut shell charcoal, which is often used in Malaysian cooking. But while it lights easily and burns hot, it does not burn long.

JAPANESE CHARCOAL The Japanese produce *binchotan*, a charcoal of incredible purity. Its uniqueness is derived from the type of hardwood used (primarily holm oak) and the method of production. Tree clippings are stacked vertically inside large kilns and charred at a relatively low temperature for two weeks. The wood is then heated to a high temperature (above 1000°C/1800°F) until the smoke is clear, signifying that all impurities have been burnt away. It is then rapidly cooled. During this process the bark is completely incinerated, and pyroligneous acid, or wood vinegar, is eliminated. The result is nearly 100 per cent pure carbon, which burns steadily and without smoke for an extended time. Binchotan should not be confused with *ogatan*, which are charcoal briquettes made from compressed sawdust.

WOOD AND THE ENVIRONMENT

Wood comes from living, growing trees, making it a renewable material. Wood burning is part of the natural carbon cycle. While burning sustainable wood is not 'carbon neutral' it can be at least considered 'carbon offset'. The carbon dioxide emitted when wood fuel is burned is the same amount that was absorbed over the years the plant was growing.

The environmental effect of wood burning depends very much on how it is done. Ethical management of our forests, the primary source of the wood we use, ensures a continual supply of wood to meet our present and future needs. As long as new plants continue to grow in place of those used for fuel, the process is sustainable. In many parts of Australia, and other parts of the world, large areas of forest are managed primarily for the continued production of wood.

At Firedoor, we work with our suppliers to source wood that would otherwise be wasted, while working with our olive oil, fruit, nut and wine producers to harvest the prunings. The ashes are recycled either to enrich the soil for growing vegetables or for use in glazing the ceramics that are produced for the restaurant.

SOURCING WOOD

Gathering wood from local forests, while exciting, is not a viable option for many of us.

Though you can get wood from the service station, it is far from ideal as it is mostly kiln-dried and fails to replicate the maturation process of open-air seasoning.

If you're going to get all fired up, it is worth sourcing premium hardwoods from recognised suppliers. At the restaurant we source the majority of our wood from Michael and Christa McDonald of Blackheath Firewood in the Blue Mountains, New South Wales. They source wood from all over Australia and will even split and stack wood to your requirements. Look online for your local supplier.

If you are lucky enough to have fruit trees, store all your cuttings for use the following year, or offer to pick up fallen branches from a local orchard or olive grove.

Wood varieties

The wood varieties table on the following pages lists a range of woods, their characteristics and what I feel are their best applications. The list is by no means exhaustive, but demonstrates the wide range of wood that can be used to fuel your fire. Wood is characterised by its flavour profile, level of heat radiation and amount of smoke emitted.

In general terms, the greater the density (kg/m^3) of the wood when dry (as shown in the table), the hotter and longer it will burn. If you are planning to cook at a very high heat or over a long period of time, you should use a denser wood. This is helpful if you are planning to cook a whole animal. If you only require a lower temperature or are cooking over a shorter period of time, a less dense wood will be sufficient. Examples of this can be found in many of the seafood recipes throughout this book.

As with any ingredient, wood is mostly a matter of personal choice. However, it is worthwhile putting some thought into which woods should be teamed with which foods. Consider the flavour strength of your food and aim to match this with a wood that has a complimentary flavour strength. The flavour itself might be quite different to the wood from which it is derived – so while nectarine wood does not taste of the fruit, it will deliver a much lighter and sweeter tone than a more robust wood, such as oak.

GENUS	COMMON NAME	DESCRIPTION	APPROX. DENSITY	APPLICATION
MYRTACEAE FAMILY				
Eucalyptus	Eucalyptus	With over 800 species, the eucalypt family is large and diverse, adapting to Australia's intense and unique environment.	850–1200	Some varieties may have a slightly resinous, medicinal smell due to the gums contained within, making them less than ideal for cooking but an excellent source of slow-burning heat. Mallee, ironbark, jarrah and red gum are all species of eucalypt suitable for grilling
	Ironbark	Probably the best Australian native wood, its dense structure provides a high temperature, long-burning wood. Its name 'ironbark' comes from the tendency of the tree to not shed its bark annually like many other eucalypts, resulting in an accumulation of dead bark. This layer of bark protects the living tissue inside the tree from fires.	1120	Suited to a wide variety of applications and an ideal base to combine with lighter, more aromatic woods
	Jarrah	Native to Western Australia. Forms dense, intensely flavoured coals.	835	Pork, beef and aged lamb
	Mallee	Slow growing, tough trees with thick roots that burn with a long and intense heat. Mallees have many stems that rise from a large bulbous woody structure called a lignotuber, or mallee root. Has a rich, earthy characteristic.	1100	Root vegetables, tubers, mushrooms as well as offal, aged beef and lamb
	Red gum	Found along the banks of watercourses, which give it a higher moisture content. Once seasoned, red gum is a good burning wood.	900	Pork, beef and smoking small goods
PROTEACEAE FAMILY				
Banksia	Banksia	Dried banksia cones burn hot with little flame and a subtle smoky aroma.	n/a	Fish, pork and poultry
Macadamia	Macadamia	Emits little heat, but produces an enticing ripe smokiness.	705	Shellfish
BETULACEAE FAMILY				
Alnus	Alder	Subtle smoke with light sweetness. Gives off little heat and burns briefly so only use for short cooking times over a medium heat.	450	Good for many fish requiring a delicate heat and only a short time to cook
Betula	Birch	Honeyed and caramel notes due to its high sugar content. Produces a good, even heat but also burns briefly like alder.	670	Fruit, pork and oily fish
Corylus	Hazel	Produces low flame, but rich smoke.	625	Pork, goat and poultry

OLEACEAE FAMILY

Olea	Olive	Lighter wood with a high erratic flame.	990	New season lamb, fruits and vegetables such as peppers, tomatoes and eggplants (aubergines)

GENUS	COMMON NAME	DESCRIPTION	APPROX. DENSITY	APPLICATION
Malus	Apple	One of the best firewoods. It has a heavenly sweet smell, which is great for cooking and smoking as it burns hot without giving off much flame. The flavour is mildly smoky with hints of fruity sweetness.	830	Poultry and shellfish, but will complement just about anything
Crataegus	Hawthorn	Rare but beautiful wood, burning hot with a gentle flame and a nutty flavour.	785	Pork, poultry, vegetables and white fish
Prunus	Almond	Very hard with long-lasting high heat and a sweet smoky flavour, complements almost all types of meat.	750	White meat, fish and vegetables
	Apricot	Beautiful burning wood with a sweet and mild flavour profile.	745	Poultry, pork and shellfish
	Cherry	Fragrant. Burns hot with a low flame.	600	Pork, duck, foie gras, fruit and chocolate
	Nectarine	Rich and sweet in flavour.	735	Poultry, pork, shellfish and fruits
	Peach	Burns slowly with a large flame and a sweet perfume over a long time.	720	Poultry, pork, shellfish, and fruits
	Plum	A good burning wood.	900	Chocolate, fruit, pork and dairy
Pyrus	Pear	Outstanding firewood, similar to apple, offering a gentle sweetness.	700	Pork, poultry, shellfish, vegetables and fruit

ROSACEAE FAMILY

GENUS	COMMON NAME	DESCRIPTION	APPROX. DENSITY	APPLICATION
Citrus	Grapefruit	A mild wood that produces a subtle smoky flavour.	590	Shellfish, such as clams and cockles
	Lemon	Low heat, sweet with a light citrus smoke.	810	Oily fish such as fresh anchovies or sardines, as well as tuna and kingfish
	Lime	Emits little heat, yet produces an enticing ripe smokiness.	560	Briny shellfish
	Orange	Solid wood that burns steadily with a sweet perfume.	855	Mussels, prawns and oily fish (see Lemon)

RUTACEAE FAMILY

GENUS	COMMON NAME	DESCRIPTION	APPROX. DENSITY	APPLICATION
Acacia	Gidgee	Species of acacia. More suited for charcoal than for smoking as the volatile gases have a hint of boiled cabbage, which accounts for its other name of 'stinking gidgee'.	1150	n/a
	Mulga	Rich flavour though higher moisture content produces heavy smoke .	1200	Dairy and small goods
	Wattle	In the same family as mesquite, but not as dense and does not burn as hot.	730	Pork, beef, poultry and oily fish
Glycyrrhiza	Liquorice	Hard and woody liquorice roots impart distinctive anise notes.	n/a	Sweet ingredients, fish, pork and game
Prosopis	Mesquite	Native to Mexico, with a high lignin content. Burns very hot and fast with a strong smoke. Has a distinct earthy flavour with vanilla notes.	820	Pork, beef, poultry and oily fish

FABACEAE FAMILY

CUPRESSACEAE FAMILY

GENUS	COMMON NAME	DESCRIPTION	APPROX. DENSITY	APPLICATION
Juniperus	Juniper	Branches of juniper have a rich botanical sweetness.	550	Smoking fish and shellfish

	GENUS	COMMON NAME	DESCRIPTION	APPROX. DENSITY	APPLICATION
FAGACEAE FAMILY	Castanea	Chestnut	A solid dry wood that burns intensely with little flame.	560	Mushroom and dairy
	Fagus	Beech	Slightly volatile, giving off a fair amount of sparks, making it less suitable for an indoor fireplace and cooking but more suited to smoking.	720	Seafood, smoking small goods and cheese
	Quercus	Oak	Oak is one of the best firewoods and an excellent all-round cooking wood. Solid slow-burning wood producing lots of heat with a small flame. If it is not fully seasoned (can take up to 2–3 years) the smoke can be very dense and bitter.	740–800	Pork, beef, oily fish, vegetables, fruit and cheese
		American oak	*Quercus alba* or white oak is recognisable by its lightish grey colour. Its structure is strong, fine-grained and dense.	770	Pork, beef, oily fish, vegetables, fruit and cheese
		English oak	*Quercus robur* is a slow growing hardwood, exceptionally dense and very high in tannin content.	740	Pork, beef, oily fish, vegetables, fruit and cheese
		French oak	*Quercus petraea* exhibits a finer grain as well as a richer contribution of aromatic components.	780	Pork, beef, oily fish, vegetables, fruit and cheese
		Holm oak	*Quercus ilex*, is a large evergreen oak. Its acorns are edible, giving jamon iberico its distinctive rich flavour. The holm oak is one of the top three trees used in the planting of truffles, which grow in a symbiotic relationship with the tree's roots.	800	Pork, beef, oily fish, vegetables, fruit and cheese
		Ubame oak	*Quercus phillyraeoides* is one of the hardest oaks and, as the tree of Wakayama Prefecture, is a natural choice in the production of binchotan.	800	Binchotan
		Oak whisky barrels	Whisky barrels exude a toasted smokiness, the subtle interplay of oak and whisky resulting in rich notes of vanilla and spice.	760	Pork, beef, oily fish, vegetables, fruit and cheese
		Oak wine barrels	American oak has a higher level of lactones, resulting in a bolder flavour than that produced by French oak, whilst red wine barrels contain more phenols than white ones. The flavour of oak lactones increases dramatically on charring, resulting in a strong woody and almost toasted coconut profile.	770	Pork, beef, oily fish, vegetables, fruit and cheese
JUGLANDACEAE FAMILY	Carya	Hickory	A hardwood with a high energy content that burns slowly with a high heat, emitting a strong sweet, almost smoked bacon, flavour.	770	Pork and smoking small goods
		Pecan	An excellent sweet and mild flavour similar to hickory which makes it excellent for smoking.	720	Pork and dairy

GENUS	COMMON NAME	DESCRIPTION	APPROX. DENSITY	APPLICATION
PINACEAE FAMILY				
Cedrus	Cedar	Has a rich tobacco perfume. Produces an even heat and moderate flame. Excellent for cooking and smoking.	360	Smoking. Note some cheeses are wrapped in cedar boxes
Picea	Spruce	A very sparky wood that burns quickly.	400	Kindling
Pinus	Pine	Softwood that burns readily. Resinous, so crackles and pops and leaves an oily soot. Generally overwhelming for food.	500	Kindling
SAPINDACEAE FAMILY				
Acer	Maple	Smoky but with a mellow, slightly sweet aroma and flavour. Makes a good fuel wood. Intense heat but rapid burning.	755	Pork, poultry and game birds
LAURACEAE FAMILY				
Cinnamomum	Cassia	Stripped bark from the whole tree, cassia is sweet and mild and has a delicate flavour with a warm spice note.	n/a	Fish, fruit, pork and game
EBENACEAE FAMILY				
Diopyros	Persimmon	Rare tree that burns well with a low flame and rich aroma.	777	Oily fish, beef, pork and poultry
MORACEAE FAMILY				
Morus	Mulberry	Low flame, sweet smelling smoke.	690	Chocolate, game
LAMIACEAE FAMILY				
Rosmarinus	Rosemary	Woody, perennial herb with fragrant savoury notes.	n/a	Dairy, lamb, goat and poultry
ANACARDIACEAE FAMILY				
Schinopsis	Quebracho	Derived from the Spanish *quebrar hacha*, which literally means 'axe breaker', and is among the heaviest and hardest in the world.	1235	Beef, pork and lamb
ULMACEAE FAMILY				
Ulmus	Elm	With a high moisture content, it smokes quite a bit, but still has good heat. Ideally requires long seasoning (up to 3 years) to get really dry and burn hot without too much smoke.	550	Poultry, game and cheese
VITACEAE FAMILY				
Vitis	Grapevines	Release a rich, robust and smoky aroma with a hint of tartness. Burns quickly, producing a small amount of embers.	545	Red meat and game
POACEAE FAMILY				
Zea	Corn cobs	A wood alternative. Contains high levels of xylan; exudes a sweet light smoke.	n/a	Poultry, fruit and corn
	Hay	Burns readily. Contains coumarin, a phytochemical with a vanilla-like flavour that naturally occurs in tonka beans, lavender, liquorice, strawberries, apricots, cherries, cinnamon and sweet clover.	n/a	Mackerel, sweetbreads and snails

How to use
this book

You are reliant on nature and
the ever-changing attributes
of the ingredients so you need
to learn to work with both.

WHEN COOKING WITH FIRE, you are reliant on nature and the ever-changing attributes of the ingredients, so you need to learn to work with both. Used as a guide, this book is intended to help you develop your instincts. I recommend that you read all the information before you begin to cook, and refer back at any stage while you are cooking.

The recipes are designed to highlight the importance of the quality of the ingredients and the skill of cooking with fire. While most recipes are straightforward, some are a bit more involved so it is best to read a recipe fully before you start. The recipes are categorised by type, highlighting the main ingredient, and are diverse in their nature. They are influenced by my time in Spain and in other countries, as well as Australia with its close proximity to Asia.

Your ingredients will always be unique (and their attributes can greatly alter how much is needed in a dish), so don't be afraid to adapt the recipes and techniques to suit your environment and the best ingredients you have available.

Go to the markets and be inspired by what looks good. You may find a beautiful whiting at the fish market and cook it in the same way as the Murray cod (see page 161), but find Jerusalem artichokes aren't available; so serve it with the grilled green beans (see page 85) instead. Likewise you may decide to alter a technique to suit another ingredient, such as cooking a chicken à la ficelle or baking a whole fish in clay.

Remember, too, not to get too hung up on the specific woods; instead, treat wood as you do other ingredients and feel free to experiment. Sometimes, I combine two or three varieties of wood to produce a certain heat or flavour profile.

While the variable nature of fire made it very difficult to write this book, I have tried to provide a basis from which to explore it further. I hope that this book changes your preconceptions of grilling, while opening your eyes to the possibilities of cooking with fire.

COOKING NOTES

It is easy to assume things about basic ingredients but I have specific requirements in the restaurant, even for the fundamentals. Here's what I used for the recipes in this book.

DAIRY All milk and cream is full fat and pasteurised and comes direct from the farmers. All butter is unsalted unless otherwise stated, and comes from Jersey cows; they produce a higher quality milk with a richer, more full-bodied flavour.

EGGS All eggs are free-range and medium sized (60 g/2¼ oz) unless otherwise stated.

SALT All salt is sea salt and either flaked or fleur de sel. It is important that it is not iodised. Salt is a crucial component of cooking that concentrates and enhances the flavour of food, in sweet as well as savoury dishes. The size and variety of salt that you choose and when you choose to season can have a profound effect on a finished dish.

SUGAR All sugar is raw cane sugar unless specified otherwise. Raw cane sugar is less refined and retains more color and flavour from the sugar cane, resulting in light brown crystals with an enriched caramel flavour.

WATER While water may not taste of anything, it has its own unique flavour that we can all distinguish. Hard water contains a much higher volume of minerals such as chalk, magnesium and calcium that may dramatically alter the flavour and the appearance of food. For a cleaner flavour, you should use soft or even filtered water wherever possible.

OIL Oil can be extracted from many different sources and is a fundamental ingredient in the kitchen. We often use grapeseed oil as it has a high smoke point and neutral flavour profile. We also use apricot kernel, pumpkin seed and, of course, olive oil.

> I hope that this book changes your preconceptions of grilling, while opening your eyes to the possibilities of cooking with fire.

Olive oil is graded by production method, acidity content and flavour, which is subject to the variety of olive, the environment in which it grows, its relative ripeness, its harvesting and how it is pressed and processed. At the restaurant, we work closely with a local olive producer in Mudgee to ensure that we get high-quality oil at its peak. While there are many varieties of olives and oil available, below are some that I like to use.

Arbequina Originally a native variety of Spain, arbequina is a small olive with low yield but with a light fruity flavour and sweet, nutty aroma, which transfers to the palate with a melted butter-like texture. It has some similarities to the Greek varietal koroneiki and is great for delicate fish and fruit.

Picual A robust Spanish variety of olive with a fragrant nose of stone fruits and zesty citrus, which pairs well with oily fish.

Frantoio An Italian varietal with a complex aroma of fresh hay and dried herbs, but transfers to the palate with pleasant nutty characteristics and a balanced bitterness and pungency.

Correglolo Another Italian variety, which due to its sheer volume of use has been described as the 'work horse of Tuscany'. It has a brilliant green appearance and green vegetal aroma with an excellent balance of bitterness and pungency, making it a great all-purpose oil.

ACIDITY Using acidity as a seasoning in cooking is fundamental, as it provides balance and changes our perception of flavour and texture. Acidity can come from many sources, from vinegars and kombucha (naturally fermented from wine or fruit) to fresh fruit such as citrus, rhubarb, gooseberries and even tomatoes. It is also found in fermented milk products, such as whey, buttermilk and yoghurt, which naturally develop lactic acid. It is important that you choose a type of acidity that will complement and enhance the flavour of your food.

TABLESPOON MEASUREMENTS Australian 20 ml (¾ fl oz) tablespoon measures are used in the recipes, so cooks with 15 ml (½ fl oz) tablespoons should be generous with their tablespoon measurements.

CUP MEASUREMENTS Metric cup measurements are used, i.e. 250 ml (8½ fl oz) for 1 cup; in the US a cup is 237 ml (8 fl oz), so American cooks should be generous with their cup measurements; in the UK, a cup is 284 ml (9½ fl oz), so British cooks should be scant with their cup measurements.

HEAT
Generally the recipes include a recommended heat level, typically defined by the intensity of the embers. Refer to the fire life cycle graph and guide on pages 42–3. This illustrates the stages of fire and will help you understand how to recognise and achieve the desired heat for each recipe. Some recipes specify a particular temperature for a wood-fired oven, which is best measured using a laser thermometer. Where the temperature in a saucepan is specified, use a sugar thermometer.

EQUIPMENT
You will need basic kitchen equipment and the following basic equipment for cooking over fire: fire poker, fire shovel, tongs, spray bottle and gloves. If a recipe calls for additional equipment, such as grill racks, clay or a wood-fired oven, this is noted above the ingredients.

SAFETY
Fire is a cruel mistress. Remember safety whenever you're dealing with her. Never leave a fire unattended, and respect total fire bans and council regulations about lighting fires outside. Don't let a fire get out of hand. Don't put too much wood on the fire at once. Always keep a bucket of water or sand nearby for smothering and extinguishing fires.

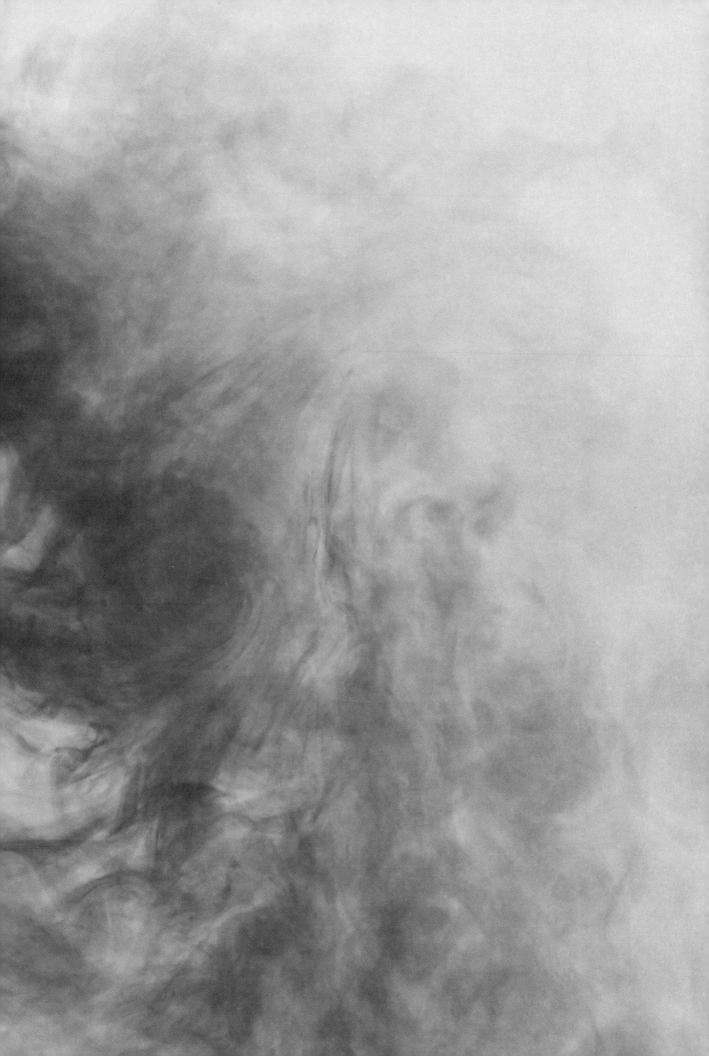

001

Vegetables

Baby cos
anchovies, smoked egg yolk

SERVES 4

Here the essential components of a caesar salad are re-created on the grill with the baby cos lettuce taking on a slight char and an amazing sweetness, which balances with the saltiness of the anchovies, the crisp capers and the richness of the egg-anchovy cream.

1. Prepare your embers and arrange a grill approximately 5 cm (2 in) above the embers.

2. Prepare the egg cream. In a small saucepan, heat the smoked oil to 68°C (160°F). Carefully add the egg yolks one at a time and cook for approximately 15 minutes, or until the eggs are just cooked. Remove the eggs using a slotted spoon, being careful not to break the yolk. Place into a clean bowl and whisk continuously, gradually adding the anchovy oil in a steady stream to form an emulsion. Add the vinegar and season with sea salt to taste.

3. Brush the sourdough with olive oil and garlic, and grill over medium embers until lightly toasted. Remove, allow to cool and blend to a coarse crumb. Season.

4. Spray the cos lettuce halves lightly with olive oil and grill for approximately 2 minutes on each side. Remove, and season with salt and the lemon zest.

5. Grill the lemon halves, cut side down, over medium embers for 3 minutes until charred and caramelised.

6. In a small cast-iron pan, fry the chilli and the capers in the olive oil until crisp.

7. Dress the cos in the grilled lemon juice and the chilli-caper oil.

8. Drape an anchovy fillet over each cos half, spoon over the egg cream, and finish with the crisp capers, parsley and the toasted sourdough crumbs.

RECIPE TYPE *savoury*

WOOD TYPE
apple wood

HEAT
medium embers

ADDITIONAL EQUIPMENT
grill, sugar thermometer, cast-iron pan

INGREDIENTS

1 slice sourdough bread

80 ml (2½ fl oz/⅓ cup) extra-virgin olive oil, plus extra for spraying

1 garlic clove, crushed

sea salt

2 baby cos (romaine) lettuce, halved

zest of ½ lemon

1 lemon, halved

½ red chilli, finely sliced

20 g (¾ oz) capers in oil, drained

8 anchovies in oil

¼ bunch flat-leaf (Italian) parsley, finely sliced

For the egg cream

300 ml (10 fl oz) Smoked oil (page 241)

3 fresh free-range egg yolks

75 ml (2½ fl oz) anchovy oil (from the tin of anchovies in oil)

1 tablespoon cava vinegar or white-wine vinegar

sea salt

NOTE

It is important to use high-quality anchovies as there are many imposters. At the restaurant, we use traditional cantabrian ones that are preserved in salt for a minimum of 8 months.

Peas

mint, jamon

SERVES 4

The Basque country, while well known for the quality of its meat and seafood, also produces the best peas in the world. The coastline has the perfect micro-climate to produce peas of intense sweetness balanced with a delicate salinity. Here the peas only grow for a short time during the month of May. They are known as *lagrimas* (tear drops), or vegetable caviar, due to their delicate nature, which means they pop in the mouth. Immature baby peas appear tear-shaped and this is when they are at their sweetest (see Note).

Grilling peas whole in their shells protects them and imbues them with the flavour from the embers. Although you don't get a lot of juice from the pods, it is sweet and intense. The combination of pea and ham is classic, but the incorporation of jamon imparts a rich flavour and intense aroma that is unparalleled. This ham undergoes extensive curing, for as long as 36 months. It has a unique sweetness, created in part by the diet of acorns the pigs feed on.

1. Prepare your embers and arrange a grill cooling rack approximately 10 cm (4 in) above the embers.

2. Grill the whole peas in their pods over the medium embers for 1–2 minutes, turning once. Remove and pod the peas, reserving the shells.

3. Juice the pea shells in a juicer and pass through a fine-mesh sieve. Reserve.

4. In a warm pan, combine the peas with the pea juices and torn mint. Season lightly with salt.

5. Warm the jamon on the grill cooling rack until it becomes translucent.

6. Divide the peas and jamon between warmed serving bowls, finish with the pea shoots and serve immediately.

RECIPE TYPE *savoury*

WOOD TYPE
olive

HEAT
medium embers

ADDITIONAL EQUIPMENT
grill cooling rack

INGREDIENTS

1.2 kg (2 lb 10 oz) fresh sugar-snap peas in their pods (see Note)

1 handful of mint leaves, torn

sea salt

100 g (3½ oz) jamon iberico, thinly sliced

young pea shoots

NOTE

For the best flavour use small peas that are young, sweet and tender.

Green beans
roasted almond cream

SERVES 4

Green beans are ideally suited to grilling as their fleshy texture results in a lightly charred and smoky exterior, while they retain tenderness within. Dressed simply in lemon, olive oil and salt, they are enriched by a roasted almond cream, which is lightened with cucumber juice for a light, summery finish.

1. Prepare your embers.

2. Prepare the almond cream. Split and roast the almonds in a dry cast-iron pan over the fire until golden brown and lightly smoky. Toss at regular intervals to ensure the almonds are evenly toasted.

3. Roast the garlic. Wrap the garlic cloves in aluminium foil. Place in the hot ashes at the edge of the fire and leave to roast for approximately 20 minutes until soft. Carefully remove from the ashes and, once cool enough to handle, squeeze the garlic from its skin.

4. In a blender, combine 50 g (1¾ oz/⅓ cup) of the roasted almonds, the almond milk, almond oil and roasted garlic until creamy. Add another 50 g (1¾ oz/⅓ cup) of the almonds and blend to a crunchy texture. Add the cucumber juice, and season with vinegar. Reserve.

5. Place the grill cooling rack over intense embers. Grill the beans for 2 minutes, turning halfway through cooking, until lightly charred yet still green.

6. Transfer the beans to a clean bowl, season with sea salt, add the lemon zest and juice, the pea tendrils and the olive oil. Toss well.

7. Divide the almond cream between serving plates, place the grilled beans on top, finish with the remaining toasted almonds and garlic flowers. Serve immediately.

RECIPE TYPE *savoury*

WOOD TYPE
olive

HEAT
intense embers

ADDITIONAL EQUIPMENT
cast-iron pan, grill cooling rack

INGREDIENTS

500 g (1 lb 2 oz) green beans, topped and tailed

sea salt

zest and juice of ½ lemon

100 g (3½ oz) pea tendrils

100 ml (3½ fl oz) fruity, mild extra-virgin olive oil, such as arbequina or koroneiki

a few white garlic flowers

For the almond cream

150 g (5½ oz/1 cup) blanched almonds

2 garlic cloves, skin on

60 ml (2 fl oz/¼ cup) almond milk

40 ml (1¼ fl oz) almond oil

juice of ¼ telegraph (long) cucumber, skin removed

2 tablespoon cava vinegar or white-wine vinegar (or to taste)

Calçots

romesco

Calçots are a variety of spring onion that have been forced to shoot like a young leek and are harvested in the spring. They originated in Spain, where people celebrate the harvest with a *calçotada*; the calçots are charred extensively over a hot fire of vine shoots, before being wrapped in newspaper and allowed to gently steam.

My first experience of this was at Mugaritz when, due to my friend working there at the time, I was invited to join their staff celebrations. Warm parcels of newspapers flanked the long tables and we were invited to uncover the humble vegetables, magically transformed by fire. Peeling back the charred exterior with our fingers uncovered a sweet and smoky interior, which we savoured with a rich romesco sauce and a barrel of the local apple cider.

1. Prepare your embers and arrange a grill directly over the top.

2. Prepare the romesco. Roast the hazelnuts in a dry cast-iron pan over the fire until golden and caramelised. Remove and cool completely.

3. Roast the garlic. Wrap the garlic cloves in aluminium foil and season with sea salt. Place in the hot ashes at the edge of the fire and leave to roast for approximately 20 minutes until soft. Carefully remove from the ashes and, once cool enough to handle, squeeze the garlic from its skin.

4. Raise the grill 5 cm (2 in) above the embers. Grill the red peppers, turning frequently until blackened all over. Transfer to a bowl or tray, cover with a lid or cloth and allow to steam and cool for 10 minutes. Carefully peel the peppers and remove the seeds.

5. Blanch the nyora pepper in a saucepan of boiling water until rehydrated. Drain and scrape the internal flesh with a spoon and reserve.

6. Blend the nyora pepper flesh with the roasted peppers, tomato water, 80 g (2¾ oz) of the toasted hazelnuts, roasted garlic, vinegar, olive oil and pimento. Season with sea salt.

7. Prepare the calçots or leeks by splitting and washing them thoroughly. Leave to soak in water for 20 minutes.

8. Drain the calçots and place directly onto the hot embers, turning until they are charred and blackened all over. Remove and wrap tightly in newspaper, leaving them to steam for 20 minutes.

9. Serve, instructing your guests to unwrap the calçots and peel their charred exteriors to reveal creamy hearts. The sweet hearts can be dipped in the fiery romesco sauce and topped with the remaining toasted hazelnuts. Savour immediately.

RECIPE TYPE *savoury*

WOOD TYPE
grapevines

HEAT
intense embers

ADDITIONAL EQUIPMENT
grill, cast-iron pan

INGREDIENTS

12 calçots or medium leeks

For the romesco

120 g (4½ oz) hazelnuts, peeled and halved

2 garlic cloves

200 g (7 oz) bull's horn red peppers

1 dried nyora pepper

100 ml (3½ fl oz) Tomato water (page 240)

40 ml (1¼ fl oz) red-wine vinegar

100 ml (3½ fl oz) extra-virgin olive oil such as arbequino or koroneiki

1 tablespoon pimento (smoked paprika)

sea salt

NOTE

Nyora (*nora*) peppers are a Spanish variety that have glossy and crimson-hued skin. The peppers are sweet, mildly hot and aromatic.

VEGETABLES

Corn
kaffir lime butter, green chilli

SERVES 4

Grilled corn is the flavour and the colour of summer: yellow, sunny and sweet. As a child, I remember playing hide and seek in the cornfields, marvelling at the towering stalks of green. Corn is a vegetable that epitomises agriculture and human intervention, as it does not exist in the wild.

Peeling back the husks after cooking reveals a transformation by fire. The vegetable's natural sweetness is enhanced by grilling in the husks, which protect the corn while imbuing a rich smoky flavour. In this recipe, the barbecued kernels are drenched in smoked butter infused with fragrant kaffir lime, and the green jalapeño provides a bitter riff to the sweetness of the corn.

1. Prepare your embers.

2. Place the corn directly on the burning embers, rotating until evenly blackened on the outside. Transfer to a clean tray.

3. Grill the onion until lightly charred and caramelised. Reserve to use in the stock.

4. Reserving 2 corncobs for grilling, cut all the kernels away from the remaining corn to total 400 g (14 oz). Reserve the cobs, cutting each in half.

5. Place the charred onion and corn cobs in a small saucepan with the water, and bring to the boil. Skim the surface of any scum and allow the stock to simmer for 10 minutes. Remove from the heat, add 2 kaffir lime leaves and allow to infuse for 10 minutes. Strain through a fine-mesh sieve into a pan.

6. Add the corn kernels to the hot stock, and simmer for 10 minutes until soft. While warm, blend in a food processor or blender on medium-high speed to form a smooth cream. Season with salt, pass through a fine-mesh sieve and reserve.

7. In a cast-iron pan, heat the grapeseed oil to 140°C (285°F). Add the jalapeños and fry until just crisp. They should remain vibrant and green. Strain off the oil and immediately transfer to a paper towel to drain. Season.

8. Finely slice the remaining kaffir lime leaves, and place in a small pan with the butter. Heat gently to melt the butter and leave to infuse for 30 minutes on a low heat. Add the lime juice.

9. Suspend the grill approximately 10 cm (4 in) above the embers. Brush the 2 whole corncobs lightly with the butter and grill until golden brown and nutty. Rotate the corn until evenly toasted, seasoning while turning.

10. Remove the corn from the heat, trim the ends and halve each cob. Roll in the kaffir lime butter.

11. Divide the corn cream between serving plates. Place one piece of corn on the cream, top with grated lime zest and crisp green jalapeños. Serve immediately.

RECIPE TYPE *savoury*

WOOD TYPE
olive

HEAT
medium-intense embers

ADDITIONAL EQUIPMENT
sugar thermometer, cast-iron pan, grill

INGREDIENTS

6 medium corncobs, husks on (see Note)

1 medium onion, halved, skin on

500 ml (17 fl oz/2 cups) filtered water

5 kaffir lime leaves

sea salt

200 ml (7 fl oz) grapeseed oil

2 green jalapeños, deseeded and finely sliced

150 g (5½ oz) Smoked butter (page 227)

zest and juice of 1 lime

NOTE

Choose ears of corn that are heavy for their size with firm kernels running all the way up to the pale golden silks at the tip.

Okra
roasted chilli, ginger and garlic

SERVES 4

Okra, also known as ladies fingers, releases mucilage upon cooking, giving the dish gumbo its thickened texture as well as its name. Unless it is required for thickening a soup or a stew, this slimy texture is less than desirable, so okra benefits from being cooked quickly. The intense heat of the grill is ideal, as the resulting okra is gently charred and verdant. Its relatively mild flavour makes it an ideal vehicle to carry the smoky flavour of the embers and the slight bitter quality of the inner seeds is sweetened by the caramelised chilli, garlic and ginger.

1. Make an ice bath, sitting a metal bowl in it to cool.

2. Prepare the aromatic oil. In a small saucepan, heat the grapeseed oil to 100°C (210°F) and fry the chilli flakes, ginger and garlic until just golden brown.

3. Remove from the heat and immediately pour into the metal bowl to cool (see Note). Season with sea salt. Place in a clean container and leave to infuse for 6 hours or overnight – this results in a much more rounded flavour.

4. In a pan, heat the grapeseed oil to 140°C (285°F) and fry the fresh chilli until crisp. Remove, season and drain on paper towel.

5. Prepare your embers until glowing and bright. Suspend the grill cooling rack approximately 5 cm (2 in) over the embers.

6. Grill the okra over intense heat for approximately 2 minutes on either side, or until lightly charred, seasoning as you turn them. Immediately transfer to a clean bowl and combine with the aromatic oil.

7. Serve immediately, garnished with the fried chilli threads.

RECIPE TYPE *savoury*

WOOD TYPE
olive

HEAT
intense embers

ADDITIONAL EQUIPMENT
sugar thermometer, grill cooling rack

INGREDIENTS

100 ml (3½ fl oz) grapeseed oil

1 fresh red chilli, deseeded and finely sliced

sea salt

300 g (10½ oz) okra

For the aromatic oil

100 ml (3½ fl oz) grapeseed oil

large pinch of dried chilli flakes

20 g (¾ oz) ginger, peeled and finely chopped

20 g (¾ oz) garlic, peeled and finely chopped

sea salt

NOTES

The ginger and chilli oil needs time to infuse, so begin the recipe at least 6 hours ahead of time.

Once the ginger and garlic are caramelised, it is important to cool the mixture immediately to arrest the cooking process; this ensures the end result is sweet and nutty, and not bitter. The flavoured oil will last up to 3 months if stored in a cool cupboard.

Beetroot
black sesame

SERVES 4

Black sesame offers a rich, sweet, earthy nuttiness that mirrors the flavour of roasted beetroot (beets). This recipe celebrates the whole vegetable – incorporating the juice, the leaves and the stem, ensuring that nothing is wasted – while adding texture and flavour.

1. Prepare your embers.

2. Prepare the beetroot by removing and reserving the stems and leaves. Wash the beetroot thoroughly.

3. Roast 4 beetroot, stem side down, in hot ashes for 1 hour, or until a metal skewer slides through easily. Remove the beetroot from the ashes and allow to cool briefly. Place more wood on the fire to produce embers for grilling and arrange a grill cooling rack approximately 10 cm (4 in) above the embers.

4. Prepare the beetroot reduction. Juice the remaining 4 beetroot and pass the juice through a fine-mesh sieve. Bring to the boil in a saucepan, add the juniper berries and black peppercorns, and reduce by two-thirds until it is the consistency of syrup. Add the vinegar, season with salt and pass through a fine-mesh sieve. Reserve.

5. Brush off any excess ash from the beetroot and, while warm, remove and discard the skin, which should come away with a gentle push of your fingers. Place the beetroot into the reduction. Set aside.

6. Prepare the sweet-pickled stems. Combine the water, vinegar, sugar and juniper berry in a small saucepan and bring to the boil, stirring to dissolve the sugar. Cut the reserved beetroot stems into small cubes, place in a clean container and pour over the hot pickle mixture. Leave for at least 20 minutes.

7. In a clean pan, gently heat the black sesame until lightly toasted (because they are black, you will have to rely on your sense of smell and be careful not to burn them). They should be nutty and fragrant. Remove and, while warm, blend the seeds in a food processor to form a paste. While still blending, pour in the olive oil in a constant stream. Add the chickpeas, yoghurt, lime zest and juice, and blend to form a cream – the consistency should be smooth, like hummus. Season with sea salt to taste.

8. Remove the beetroot from the reduction and cut each one in half. Grill on the grill cooling rack over hot embers until coloured on all sides.

9. Grill the beetroot leaves on the grill cooling rack over the embers until just crisp. Season with sea salt.

10. Serve the beetroot with the black sesame cream, grilled leaves and pickled stems. Drizzle over the beetroot reduction and finish with freshly grated lime zest.

RECIPE TYPE *savoury*

WOOD TYPE
ironbark

HEAT
hot ash, medium-intense embers

ADDITIONAL EQUIPMENT
grill cooling rack

INGREDIENTS

8 medium beetroot (beets), stems and leaves attached

2 juniper berries, crushed with the back of a spoon

4 black peppercorns

20 ml (¾ fl oz) aged red-wine vinegar

sea salt

60 g (2 oz) black sesame seeds

50 ml (1¾ fl oz) arbequina olive oil

100 g (3½ oz) cooked chickpeas

40 g (1½ oz) Greek yoghurt

zest and juice of ½ lime, plus extra zest for serving

For the sweet pickle

50 ml (1¾ fl oz) filtered water

50 ml (1¾ fl oz) red-wine vinegar

50 g (1¾ oz) sugar

1 juniper berry, crushed with the back of a spoon

Asparagus
mussel cream, rye

SERVES 4

Growing up in the UK, I would always look forward to the English green asparagus season. It just tastes better than any asparagus in the world. Signalling the onset of spring, the brief availability of asparagus made it a short-lived seasonal treat.

Its natural sweetness soon dissipates after harvesting, which is why asparagus that has to travel from the other side of the world just isn't the same. Asparagus is best eaten with the fingers and I encourage you to dip each spear in the rich mussel cream, the flavour of which is heightened by the burnt orange powder and the crunch of the toasted rye crumbs.

1. Prepare your embers and arrange a grill cooling rack directly over the top.

2. Remove the peel from the orange, being careful to remove all traces of pith from the skin. Juice the orange and reserve. Toast the orange skin on the grill cooling rack 20 cm (8 in) above the embers. Remove from the embers, allow to cool and, using a mortar and pestle, pound to a fine powder Reserve.

3. Toast the rye bread on the grill cooling rack over the embers. Remove, allow to cool, then blend in a food processor to a coarse crumb. Season with sea salt.

4. Spread the embers evenly across the base of the grate and set the grill cooling rack close to the burning embers (approximately 2.5 cm/1 in).

5. Place the mussels on one side directly on the grill. Cover with a deep heatproof pan (to act as a lid) and cook for 2–3 minutes.

6. Using a pair of tongs, carefully transfer the mussels to a clean dish as they open, conserving as much of their juices as possible. Strain the juice into a saucepan.

7. Set the mussel juices over a medium heat and add the reserved orange juice. Reduce the liquid by half.

8. Remove the mussels from their shells, removing any beards with a small knife. In a food processor, blend the mussels to a smooth cream with the mussel-orange reduction and the olive oil. Pass through a fine-mesh sieve, chill and reserve.

9. Prepare the asparagus by breaking off the woody ends. Grill on the grill cooling rack 5 cm (2 in) above the embers for 3–4 minutes until tender and slightly charred. Remove and, while still warm, season with the lemon zest and juice, and a drizzle of olive oil.

10. Place the asparagus alongside a spoon of the mussel cream dusted with the toasted orange powder. Garnish the asparagus with the grilled rye crumbs and the agretti. Serve immediately.

RECIPE TYPE *savoury*

WOOD TYPE
orange, olive

HEAT
intense embers

ADDITIONAL EQUIPMENT
grill cooling rack

INGREDIENTS

1 orange

2 slices dark rye bread

sea salt

500 g (1 lb 2 oz) live mussels, cleaned (see Note, page 141)

100 ml (3½ fl oz) fruity, mild extra-virgin olive oil, such as arbequina or koroneiki, plus extra for the asparagus

4 bunches asparagus spears

zest and juice of ½ lemon

100 g (3½ oz) agretti (see Notes)

NOTES

For the best flavour, only use asparagus when in season. Fresh asparagus should be firm with a tight and compact head forming a neat point at the end.

A Mediterranean native, agretti is also known as land seaweed or saltwort. Its salty succulence may also be substituted with samphire or karkalla.

Broccoli
eggplant, fermented chilli brittle

SERVES 4

Broccoli develops a beautiful sweet nuttiness when grilled and pairs particularly well with the creamy smokiness of the eggplant purée in this dish.

The fermented chilli brittle provides a bit of heat and a welcome crunch, too.

1. Prepare your embers.

2. In a medium saucepan, heat 200 ml (7 fl oz) of the peanut oil to 180°C (355°F). Fry the peanuts in the oil until lightly browned. Strain and place the peanuts on paper towel to drain, reserving the oil. Repeat the process with the pumpkin seeds.

3. In a small saucepan, heat the remaining peanut oil and fry the fermented chilli paste until the moisture has evaporated. Add the sugar and water, and continue to heat until the mixture reaches 150°C (300°F) (hard crack stage) on a sugar thermometer. Mix in the nuts and seeds, pour onto a clean baking tray and allow to cool completely. Once the nuts and seeds have cooled, break the brittle into small pieces and reserve.

4. Spread the embers evenly across the base of the grate and set the grill cooling rack 5 cm (2 in) above the burning embers. Pinprick the eggplants all over and place directly on the grill over an intense heat so that the skin blisters and blackens, rotating to ensure that it blisters evenly.

5. Remove the eggplants from the rack, allow to rest for 5 minutes, then carefully remove the charred skin. Place the flesh of the eggplants on a clean dish, season and drizzle with the reserved peanut oil. The smoky juices of the eggplant should run and mingle with the oil.

6. In a food processor, blend the eggplant with its juices and the rice vinegar until smooth and creamy. Season with sea salt and pass through a fine-mesh sieve.

7. In a cast-iron pan, heat the grapeseed oil to 140°C (285°F) and fry the chilli until crisp. Remove the fried chilli with a slotted spoon, season and drain on paper towel.

8. Prepare the broccoli by peeling the woody base stems, reserving the leaves and cutting the head into eighths. Grill the broccoli for 3–4 minutes until lightly charred. Turn to repeat on the other side. Transfer to a clean tray, season well with sea salt and lime zest, and drizzle lightly with olive oil.

9. Grill the broccoli leaves quickly over the embers until crisp and toasted. Season.

10. Arrange the broccoli on the warm eggplant purée, and garnish with the toasted broccoli leaves, crumbled nut brittle and chilli threads. Serve immediately.

RECIPE TYPE *savoury*

WOOD TYPE
olive

HEAT
medium-intense embers

ADDITIONAL EQUIPMENT
sugar thermometer, grill cooling rack, cast-iron pan

INGREDIENTS

250 ml (8½ fl oz/1 cup) peanut oil

100 g (3½ oz) peanuts

25 g (1 oz) pumpkin seeds (pepitas)

2 teaspoons Fermented chilli paste (page 242)

30 g (1 oz) coconut sugar

80 ml (2½ fl oz/⅓ cup) filtered water

2 large eggplants (aubergines)

35 ml (1¼ fl oz) rice vinegar

sea salt

200 ml (7 fl oz) grapeseed oil

1 red chilli, deseeded and finely sliced

1 large whole head of broccoli

zest of 1 lime

extra-virgin olive oil, to drizzle

Brussels sprouts
smoked ham hock, potatoes

SERVES 4

Brussels sprouts can be very divisive, with our love–hate relationship apparently stemming from a genetic sensitivity to bitterness, found in approximately half of the population. Either way, boiling the sprouts to death does them no favours, releasing lots of unpleasant sulphur. Like all vegetables, they are best eaten as soon as possible after harvesting and grilling them helps to develop a sweet, nutty richness that is hard to resist whatever your genetic make-up.

There is something about smoked ham hocks I take comfort in; they are rich, smoky and salty. Each year in the restaurant we work with a local smokehouse to smoke batches of free-range pork hocks that are sourced from a single family–owned farm on the Darling Downs. The 10,000 acres of fertile pasture ensure that the pigs can forage around finding food in a stress-free environment, which makes for better tasting pork. The creaminess of the potato rounds the dish, which rides a beautiful balance between bitter, sweet and salty.

1. Prepare your embers.

2. Preheat your wood-fired oven to 200°C (390°F). Roast the ham hock in the oven for 10–15 minutes until golden brown.

3. In a large flameproof casserole dish, add the ham hock, stock, white wine, onion, carrot and celery. Braise either on the stovetop or in the wood-fired oven at 120°C (250°F) for 2–3 hours until the meat is falling off the bone. Allow to cool, strain the stock into a jug, remove and discard the vegetables, and pull the meat off the bone. Place the ham into a cast-iron pan and cover with the strained stock. Set aside.

4. Meanwhile, wash and thoroughly dry the potatoes. Spread the salt out on a baking tray that is large enough to hold the potatoes in a single layer. Arrange the potatoes on top and bake in the wood-fired oven at 200°C (390°F) for 50 minutes until the potatoes are tender in the middle. Remove and peel while warm, breaking the potatoes into even pieces. Set aside.

5. Carefully remove the outer leaves of the brussels sprouts and reserve. Cut the hearts in half. Spray lightly with olive oil and grill on a grill cooling rack set 15 cm (6 in) above the embers (or roast in the wood-fired oven at 200°C/390°F for 10 minutes) until golden. Season lightly, scatter the reserved sprout leaves on top and cook for a further 4 minutes until crisp.

6. In a medium saucepan, warm the potatoes and ham in the stock. Divide between serving bowls and cover with the roasted brussels sprouts and leaves.

RECIPE TYPE	*savoury*

WOOD TYPE
ironbark

HEAT
intense embers

ADDITIONAL EQUIPMENT
wood-fired oven, laser thermometer, cast-iron pan, grill cooling rack

INGREDIENTS

1 × 540 g (1 lb 3 oz) smoked free-range ham hock

750 ml (25½ fl oz/3 cups) chicken stock

250 ml (8½ fl oz/1 cup) white wine

1 brown onion, halved

1 carrot, roughly chopped

2 celery stalks, roughly chopped

500 g (1 lb 2 oz) Dutch cream potatoes

475 g (1 lb 1 oz/1½ cups) rock salt

350 g (12½ oz) brussels sprouts

olive oil

sea salt

ALTERNATIVE METHOD

Roast the brussels sprouts in a cast-iron pan in a wood-fired oven.

Eggplant
shiitake, wild garlic

SERVES 4

Plump shiny eggplants char beautifully on the grill, the skin protecting the delicate flesh, which cooks slowly within. The interior turns into the texture of silky custard while gaining a smoky sweetness, which mellows the bitterness of the vegetable. Earthy, rich and full-bodied, shiitake mushrooms are rich in umami and impart a pungent, meaty flavour to the dish.

1. Prepare your embers. Spread the embers evenly across the base of the grate and arrange a grill approximately 5 cm (2 in) above the embers.

2. Pinprick the eggplants all over and place directly on the grill so that the skin blisters and blackens, rotating to ensure that it blisters evenly all over.

3. Remove from the grill and allow to rest for 5 minutes. Carefully peel away the charred skin.

4. Place the flesh of the eggplants on a clean dish, season with salt and drizzle liberally with the olive oil.

5. Allow to sit for 5-10 minutes; the smoky juices of the eggplant will run and mingle with the olive oil.

6. Meanwhile, spray the shiitake mushrooms lightly with olive oil, season with salt and grill, cap side down for 5-6 minutes until tender.

7. Grill the enoki mushrooms and the wild garlic until lightly charred.

8. Halve the eggplants lengthways and put them back on the grill to warm through, reserving the juices.

9. Serve immediately by placing half an eggplant in a shallow bowl topped with the grilled shiitake, enoki and wild garlic. Pour over the reserved eggplant juices to finish.

RECIPE TYPE *savoury*

WOOD TYPE
seasoned hardwood, preferably mallee, burnt slowly down to embers

HEAT
medium-intense embers

ADDITIONAL EQUIPMENT
grill

INGREDIENTS

2 ripe eggplants (aubergines) (see Note), green calyxes removed and stems retained

sea salt

100 ml (3½ fl oz) light, fruity olive oil such as koroneiki or arbequina, plus extra for spraying

300 g (10½ oz) shiitake mushrooms, brushed clean

100 g (3½ oz) enoki mushrooms, cleaned and divided into 8 clusters

1 bunch wild garlic

NOTE

Be sure you are buying a mature, ripe eggplant, choosing those that feel heavy for their size. Eggplants that are full of seeds indicate that the fruit is not at its peak and will have a more pronounced bitter profile. Also ensure that you prick the eggplants before placing on the fire to release the trapped steam, which may otherwise result in the eggplants exploding.

Butternut pumpkin
smoked ricotta, pepitas

SERVES 4

When buried, pumpkins hold their own deep in the ashes. The buttery and sweet slow-roasted butternut pairs well with the creamy smoked ricotta. Even the pumpkin vines are incorporated, and the toasted pepitas provide a good crunch while the toasted cereal flakes offer a worthy earthy note.

1. Prepare your embers or wood-fired oven.

2. Bury the pumpkins directly in the hot ashes surrounding the fire. Leave to cook for 50-60 minutes until a skewer passes effortlessly through the flesh. Remove from the ashes. Place more wood on the fire to produce embers for grilling.

3. Halve the pumpkins crossways and remove the seeds.

4. Heat a cast-iron pan over the fire or in a wood-fired oven at 200°C (390°F). Add 50 ml (1¾ fl oz) of the olive oil, then carefully place the pumpkin, cut side down, in the pan. Roast for 10 minutes until the sugars have caramelised, turning a rich golden brown. Turn, season and continue roasting for another 5 minutes.

5. If using, prepare the pumpkin vines by separating the tender side shoots from the fibrous main vine. Grill the pumpkin vines for 1 minute, transfer to a bowl, combine with the torn radicchio leaves and dress with sherry vinegar and the remaining olive oil.

6. Fill each butternut pumpkin half with the smoked ricotta, and top with the pumpkin vines and radicchio. Scatter with toasted pumpkin seeds and rolled oats and drizzle with pumpkin seed oil. Serve immediately.

RECIPE TYPE *savoury*

WOOD TYPE
ironbark

HEAT
hot ash, medium-intense embers

ADDITIONAL EQUIPMENT
cast-iron pan or wood-fired oven, laser thermometer

INGREDIENTS

2 small butternut pumpkins (squash)

110 ml (4 fl oz) extra-virgin olive oil

sea salt

1 bunch pumpkin vines with young leaves (optional)

½ head radicchio, leaves separated and torn

20 ml (¾ fl oz) aged sherry vinegar

250 g (9 oz) Smoked ricotta (page 224)

30 g (1 oz/¼ cup) pepitas (pumpkin seeds), toasted

30 g (1 oz) rolled oats, toasted

20 ml (¾ fl oz) pumpkin seed oil

ALTERNATIVE METHOD

Roast the pumpkin in a wood-fired oven.

Leaves
guanciale, pecans

SERVES 4

There is something about cooking lettuce that seems so wrong, and yet it tastes so right. Strangely enough – in spite of the caviar, the oysters and the other extreme things we grilled in the Basque country – when I was asked if there was anything we didn't grill at Etxebarri, I would always smile and say, 'Well, we don't grill the salad, of course'. Salad to the Spanish is sacred, so when I came to Australia not bound by the same restraint, I thought why the hell not.

We composed a salad of baby gem, radicchio and chicory, which we finished with glistening slices of warm guanciale (an Italian cured meat) and fresh pecans from my friend's farm. Grilling lettuce and bitter leaves lifts them to hero status, creating a beautiful balance of lightly charred outer leaves and a caramelised body. The radicchio softens and sweetens on the grill while the centres of the tight heads of baby gem retain a characteristic crunch.

1. Prepare your embers and arrange a grill directly on top.

2. Prepare the dressing. Combine the vinegars with the salt and, whisking continuously, gradually add the oils until emulsified.

3. Spray the split lettuce heads lightly with olive oil and grill for 2–3 minutes on each side until caramelised and lightly charred. Remove, season with salt and orange zest, and toss in the dressing.

4. Place the guanciale on a metal tray 20 cm (8 in) above the embers and gently warm until translucent.

5. Divide the leaves and guanciale between warm bowls, finish with fresh pecans broken and scattered over, and serve immediately.

RECIPE TYPE *savoury*

WOOD TYPE
apple

HEAT
medium-intense embers

ADDITIONAL EQUIPMENT
grill

INGREDIENTS

2 baby gem lettuces, halved

1 radicchio, quartered

2 chicories (endives), halved

olive oil

sea salt

zest of ½ orange

12 slices guanciale (cured pork jowl), sliced thinly

100 g (3½ oz) fresh pecans, shelled

For the dressing

2 tablespoons apple wine vinegar

2 tablespoons Pedro Ximénez vinegar

pinch of sea salt

60 ml (2 fl oz/¼ cup) grapeseed oil

60 ml (2 fl oz/¼ cup) extra-virgin olive oil

VEGETABLES

Piperade

eggs

SERVES 4

Piperade is a classic Basque dish of green peppers, tomatoes and onions, the colours of which also represent Ikurriña, the national flag: green, red and white. It is a dish of national pride and, typical of the Basque style of cooking, a simple dish that becomes something incredible thanks to the quality of the ingredients.

The dish is named after a particular variety of green pepper called the *biper eztia*. This pairs well with the vibrancy of red bull's horn peppers. Long and thin, their sweet flavour is intensified by grilling, balancing out the bitterness of the charred skin. Breaking away from tradition, both the onion and the peppers are grilled over the fire, adding further complexity to the flavours of this dish. Here, eggs are baked nestled within the piperade creating a type of *shakshuka* (loosely translated from Arabic as 'all mixed up') and resulting in a delicious one-pan meal.

1. Prepare your intense embers and arrange a grill approximately 10 cm (4 in) above the embers.

2. Prepare the peppers. Grill the green and red peppers whole, turning frequently until blackened all over. Transfer to a bowl or tray, cover with a lid or cloth and allow to steam for 10 minutes. When cool enough to handle, carefully peel and remove the seeds from the peppers and discard. Season the flesh of the peppers and cut into strips. Place in a bowl.

3. Grill the onions and the tomatoes for 10–15 minutes until tender, lightly charred and caramelised. Remove from the grill and roughly chop the onions and the tomatoes before combining with the pepper strips.

4. Heat the olive oil in a cast-iron pan and fry the garlic for 1 minute until fragrant. Add the onions, tomatoes, peppers, thyme sprig and espelette pepper and cook for 20–30 minutes until soft. Season well with sea salt.

5. Break the eggs, one at a time, directly into the pan and ensure they are evenly spaced. Cook over medium embers for 10–12 minutes, until the eggs are just beginning to set on top.

6. Divide the piperade between serving bowls. Finish with torn fresh parsley and serve immediately.

RECIPE TYPE *savoury*

WOOD TYPE
olive

HEAT
intense embers, medium embers

ADDITIONAL EQUIPMENT
grill, cast-iron pan

INGREDIENTS

2 long, thin green peppers

2 long, thin red bull's horn peppers

sea salt

2 onions, halved

6 ripe tomatoes, halved

80 ml (2½ fl oz/⅓ cup) extra-virgin olive oil

1 garlic clove, minced

1 thyme sprig

½ teaspoon espelette pepper

4 eggs, at room temperature

¼ bunch flat-leaf (Italian) parsley, torn

Potato
crème fraîche, bottarga

SERVES 4

The skin of a potato makes it ideal for baking slowly in the ashes of the fire. Breaking it into pieces once it is cooked instead of cutting it increases the surface area and roughs up the edges, which turn crunchy and golden while the inside is tender and fluffy.

1. Prepare your ashes, burning the wood slowly for 2 hours to produce hot ashes with dying embers.

2. Bury the potatoes directly in hot ashes from the fire (220-250°C/ 430-480°F). Leave the potatoes to cook for 1½ hours until the flesh beneath the skin feels soft.

3. Meanwhile, in a bowl, fold the chopped dill through the crème fraîche along with the lemon zest and juice. Season with salt and set aside.

4. Remove the potatoes from the ashes, brush off the ash dust and, using the back of a spoon, press the potatoes to break them apart.

5. Heat a cast-iron pan over intense embers, add the tallow and heat until almost starting to smoke, then add the potatoes. Cook for 5 minutes on each side until evenly browned, basting regularly with the hot fat. Continue roasting in the pan over medium embers for 10 minutes until the potato pieces are crispy.

6. Remove the potatoes with a slotted spoon and drain on paper towel. Season with sea salt.

7. Arrange the potatoes on a serving plate, spoon over the crème fraîche and grate over the bottarga. Serve immediately, garnished with fresh dill sprigs.

RECIPE TYPE *savoury*

WOOD TYPE
ironbark

HEAT
hot ashes, intense embers

EQUIPMENT
cast-iron pan

INGREDIENTS

4 × 220 g (8 oz) royal blue or other floury potatoes

½ bunch dill (reserve 8 sprigs to garnish), chopped

120 g (4½ oz) crème fraîche

zest and juice of ½ lemon

sea salt

100 g (3½ oz) dry-aged tallow (beef fat) or other rendered animal fat, such as duck fat

20 g (¾ oz) bottarga (salted mullet roe)

ALTERNATIVE METHOD

Bake the potato, then roast it in a wood-fired oven.

King brown mushrooms
raw beef, celeriac

SERVES 4

When cooked, king brown mushrooms possess a rich, robust flavour and a dense texture, but exhibit little taste when raw. Grilling enhances their woody aroma and they develop a dense, meaty quality and sweet smokiness that is packed with umami. Raw slices of dry-aged beef intensify the mushrooms' meatiness, while the celeriac provides a spicy and pungent finish.

1. Prepare your embers.

2. Prepare the celeriac purée. Lightly spray the celeriac discs on both sides with the grapeseed oil and place on the grill cooling rack 10 cm (4 in) above the embers.

3. Cook the celeriac discs on both sides until they become jet-black in colour and start to feel very soft.

4. While still hot, transfer to a blender and blitz on a medium-high speed to form a paste. With the machine still running on medium speed, gradually pour in the boiling water (you may not need all of the water) and blitz to form a smooth consistency. Add the olive oil and continue to blitz for a further 2 minutes.

5. Season and add the vinegar, adjusting to taste. Pass the purée through a fine-mesh sieve lined with muslin (cheesecloth) into a container.

6. Spray the mushrooms lightly with grapeseed oil and place on a grill cooling rack 15 cm (6 in) above the embers, cut side down. Cover and grill over the embers for 8 minutes until the juices begin to release and the mushrooms turn a honeyed brown colour. Turn the mushrooms, season, and grill for a further 4 minutes.

7. Place spoonfuls of the celeriac purée on serving plates, topping each with a mushroom half. Drape the slices of beef (1 slice per mushroom) over the mushroom halves and serve immediately.

RECIPE TYPE *savoury*

WOOD TYPE
mallee

HEAT
medium-gentle embers

ADDITIONAL EQUIPMENT
grill cooling rack

INGREDIENTS

400 g (14 oz) king brown mushrooms, cleaned and halved

grapeseed oil, for spraying

sea salt

60 g (2 oz) raw beef, preferably dry aged, thinly sliced

For the celeriac purée

200 g (7 oz) celeriac, peeled and cut into 1.5 cm (½ in) thick discs

grapeseed oil, for spraying

150–200 ml (5–7 fl oz) boiling filtered water

100 ml (3½ fl oz) olive oil

sea salt

cava vinegar, to taste

Cauliflower
tallow, hazelnuts

SERVES 4

Grilling or roasting cauliflower results in an incredible natural sweetness that, in this recipe, is enhanced by the tallow and roasted hazelnuts.

1. Prepare your embers.

2. In a cast-iron pan, gently dry roast the hazelnuts until golden brown. Remove, roll in a tea towel (dish towel) to remove the brown papery skin, then split the hazelnuts in half and reserve.

3. Cut the cauliflower head in half down the middle and brush lightly with a little of the tallow. Place on the grill. Grill for 8–10 minutes until golden brown. Transfer to a heavy-based pan with the remaining tallow, season with salt and continue to roast over the fire for a further 10–12 minutes, turning once and basting continually.

4. Pour in the vinegar and boil, stirring, to deglaze the pan, and toss in the toasted hazelnuts.

5. Place the cauliflower leaves on the grill. Grill quickly until lightly charred, and place them around the cauliflower on a serving plate.

6. Whisk together the tallow and vinegar mixture remaining in the pan, season, pour it over the cauliflower and serve immediately.

RECIPE TYPE *savoury*

WOOD TYPE
ironbark

HEAT
intense embers

ADDITIONAL EQUIPMENT
cast-iron pan, grill or wood-fired oven

INGREDIENTS

40 g (1½ oz) hazelnuts

1 head cauliflower, leaves removed and reserved

120 g (4½ oz) aged tallow (beef fat), preferably from dry-aged beef, melted, plus extra for brushing

sea salt

60 ml (2 fl oz/¼ cup) aged Pedro Ximénez vinegar

ALTERNATIVE METHOD
Roast the cauliflower in a wood-fired oven.

Cucumbers
dill, horseradish

SERVES 4

The saying 'as cool as a cucumber' refers to the vegetable's refreshing nature and high water content; they actually feel cooler than air temperature. Given the intense nature of the grill environment, it is surprising that anything could remain cool but this dish manages to do that. It is refreshing and is full of distinctive contrasts of textures and flavours – all from the cucumber. The combination of fermented and grilled cucumber, and the bracing nature of the raw cucumber, results in notes of complex char, briny tang, and unadulterated rawness in the same mouthful. The dill crème fraîche binds the cucumbers into a heavenly threesome, which is lifted by the horseradish.

1. To ferment the cucumbers, place them in a 500 ml (17 fl oz/2 cups) sterilised glass jar, adding the sliced horseradish and dill and submerging in the cold salt brine and whey. Seal tightly and leave to ferment in a cool place out of direct light for 3 days. The cucumbers will break down naturally and develop lactic acid. Once fermented, refrigerate until ready to use.

2. Prepare your embers and arrange a grill directly on the embers.

3. Remove the fermented cucumber from the brine and drain, reserving the fermented liquid.

4. In a bowl, mix the dill through the crème fraîche with 60 ml (2 fl oz/¼ cup) of the fermented cucumber liquid.

5. Grill the raw and fermented cucumbers over direct heat for approximately 2 minutes until lightly charred. Remove and drizzle with the olive oil and toss through the lemon or apple cucumber, lemon balm leaves and watercress.

6. Arrange the cucumbers on top of the dill crème fraîche and grate over the fresh horseradish to finish. Serve immediately.

RECIPE TYPE *savoury*

WOOD TYPE
olive

HEAT
medium-intense embers

ADDITIONAL EQUIPMENT
grill

INGREDIENTS

½ bunch dill, chopped

100 g (3½ oz) crème fraîche

4 baby cucumbers, halved

fruity, mild extra-virgin olive oil, such as arbequina or koroneiki

1 lemon or apple cucumber, cut into eighths

3 lemon balm leaves, chopped

1 bunch watercress, leaves picked

15 g (½ oz) fresh horseradish root, peeled

For the fermented cucumbers

4 baby cucumbers, trimmed to remove the blossom end, halved

10 g (¼ oz) horseradish root, peeled and sliced

½ bunch dill, chopped

500 ml (17 fl oz/2 cups) Salt brine, 5%, chilled (page 240)

50 ml (1¾ fl oz) whey (see Note)

NOTES

The cucumber needs time to ferment, so begin the recipe 3 days ahead of time.

Whey is the reserved liquid left over from making ricotta or butter (pages 224, 227). Alternatively, substitute the whey with 2 tablespoons buttermilk (page 227) mixed with 4 teaspoons filtered water.

Pumpkin sour

Vegetables in a cocktail? Not as crazy as it sounds. This drink combines the gentle smoke of whisky with the sweetness of the butternut pumpkin and honey. Fragrant thyme and zingy lemon bring a fresh tone to this unique and delicious drink.

1. Prepare your embers, burning the wood slowly for 1 hour.

2. Prepare the purée. Roast the butternut pumpkin directly in the embers, turning regularly until softened.

3. Remove the pumpkin from the embers, cut open and, with a spoon, remove the seeds and scoop out the flesh, avoiding the skin. Purée in a food processor. Transfer to a bowl, add the thyme sprigs and drizzle over the honey.

4. To assemble the cocktail, place the whisky, lemon juice and 45 ml (1½ fl oz) butternut pumpkin and honey purée in a cocktail shaker and shake well. Add the ice and egg white and shake a second time to chill and dilute.

5. Strain into a chilled cocktail glass and rest a sprig of lemon thyme on the rim.

RECIPE TYPE *drink*

WOOD TYPE
ironbark

HEAT
medium embers

INGREDIENTS

50 ml (1¾ fl oz) peated Scotch whisky

30 ml (1 fl oz) lemon juice

45 ml (1½ fl oz) butternut pumpkin (squash) and honey purée

ice cubes

1 egg white

1 lemon thyme sprig, to garnish

For the butternut pumpkin and honey purée

1 small butternut pumpkin (squash)

2 thyme sprigs

100 g (3½ oz) honey

Spaghetti squash
kataifi, pickled rose petals

SERVES 4

Spaghetti squash always fascinated me as a child. It has yellow flesh that, once cooked, falls away in strands resembling spaghetti and, with a little butter and salt, tastes delicious. It was a great way for my mother to introduce me to vegetables.

In Spain they eat a lot of squash in various forms, even in sweets such as *cabello d'angel* (literally translated as 'angel's hair') where the strands are cooked down with sugar and cinnamon to make a transparent jam. This recipe echoes this tradition, with the squash cooked slowly in the ashes, concentrating the flavours and caramelising the natural sugars. The strands are then lightly candied before being combined with kataifi, a shredded filo dough used to make many traditional Lebanese sweets. The kataifi mirrors the strands of the squash while providing a crisp exterior. The pickled rose petals provide a fragrant acidity against the sweet pastry.

1. Prepare the pickling liquid for the rose petals. Bring the rosewater, vinegar, sugar and salt to the boil in a saucepan. Stir to dissolve the sugar and salt, then remove from the heat and allow to cool.

2. In a separate pan, bring the water to the boil. Add the rose petals and blanch for 2-3 minutes until softened. Drain and place immediately in the rose pickling liquid. Steep for 4 hours or overnight.

3. Prepare your embers and ignite a fire in the wood-fired oven.

4. Pinprick holes in the squash and bury directly in hot ashes (at 200-220°C/390-430°F). Leave to cook for 1½ hours until the flesh beneath the skin feels soft. Remove and allow to cool.

5. On a clean tray, halve the squash, reserving any juices and, with a spoon, carefully remove the seeds. With a fork, transfer the flesh in long strands to a clean container, scraping the squash clean.

6. In a medium saucepan, heat the reserved juices, sugar, lemon zest and juice, cinnamon stick and nutmeg, and bring to the boil. Simmer for 5 minutes and allow to cool slightly before removing 100 ml (3½ fl oz) of the syrup. To the remaining syrup, add the spaghetti squash and simmer for 40-60 minutes until the strands become separated, translucent and glassy. Remove from the heat and allow to cool.

7. Take a handful of the kataifi pastry strands and spread them out lengthways on a work surface. Drizzle with smoked butter, and place 2 tablespoons of spaghetti squash at one end of the pastry. Roll up tightly, drizzling with butter. Repeat with the remaining pastry, butter and spaghetti squash.

8. Bake in the wood-fired oven for 10-20 minutes at 180°C (355°F) until the kataifi is golden, toasted and crisp. Remove and spoon over the remaining syrup.

9. Serve immediately with a tablespoon of the rose pickling liquid over each kataifi and a scattering of pickled rose petals. Finish by scattering over the sliced pistachios. Serve immediately.

RECIPE TYPE *sweet*

WOOD TYPE
nut

HEAT
hot ash, medium embers

ADDITIONAL EQUIPMENT
wood-fired oven, laser thermometer

INGREDIENTS

1 spaghetti squash, 1–1.2 kg (2 lb 3 oz–2 lb 10 oz)

400 g (14 oz) sugar

zest and juice of 1 lemon

1 cinnamon stick

grated nutmeg

200 g (7 oz) kataifi pastry

100 g (3½ oz) Smoked butter, melted (page 227)

50 g (1¾ oz/⅓ cup) fresh pistachios, sliced

For the rose petals

100 ml (3½ fl oz) rosewater

100 ml (3½ fl oz) rice vinegar

60 g (2 oz) sugar

pinch of sea salt

200 ml (7 fl oz) filtered water

2 fresh roses (pesticide free), petals picked

NOTE

The rose petals need time to steep in the picking liquid, so begin the recipe at least 4 hours ahead of time.

Sweet corn brûlée

I prefer to coax out the natural sweetness of vegetables and fruits rather than relying purely on refined sugars. Go back far enough, and you discover that the idea of savoury desserts is nothing new. Corn isn't a commonly used ingredient in dessert, but grilling accentuates everything that is good about it. The corn becomes sugary-sweet and the yellow gets even yellower, making it an ideal enhancement for a classic custard tart.

1. Prepare your wood-fired oven.

2. Place the corn directly on the burning embers, rotating until evenly blackened on the outside. Remove, allow to cool enough to handle, peel back the husks and cut off the kernels with a knife.

3. In a small saucepan, combine the cream, milk and corn kernels and bring to the boil. Transfer to a clean container and lightly blend using an electric hand blender for 30 seconds (you do not want a purée). Leave to infuse for 1 hour before straining the liquid into a jug.

4. Whisk the egg yolks and the caster sugar until pale and creamy. Whisk in the infused corn milk and pass through a fine-mesh sieve.

5. Divide the mixture between 4 ramekins or heatproof bowls (250 ml/ 8½ fl oz/1 cup capacity).

6. Bake in the wood-fired oven at 120°C (250°F) for 30-40 minutes, or until gently set with a slight wobble in the middle. Remove and allow to cool.

7. Sprinkle the top with the remaining sugar, rotating the ramekin to ensure an even spread of sugar.

8. Using a brûlée iron heated until very hot in the fire (or alternatively a blowtorch or under a hot grill/broiler) caramelise the sugar until it is a rich amber colour.

9. Finish with fresh lime zest as the custard sets and hardens. Serve immediately.

RECIPE TYPE *sweet*

WOOD TYPE
olive

HEAT
medium-gentle embers

ADDITIONAL EQUIPMENT
wood-fired oven, laser thermometer, hot iron or blowtorch

INGREDIENTS

3 large corncobs, husks on

375 ml (12½ fl oz/1½ cups) thick (double/heavy) cream

200 ml (7 fl oz) milk

4 egg yolks

80 g (2¾ oz/⅓ cup) caster (superfine) sugar

zest of ½ lime

002

Seafood

Marron

finger lime, native herbs

SERVES 4

Marron are freshwater crayfish endemic to Australia. Primarily farmed in dams, but also found in billabongs, they have a sweet, delicate, almost nutty flavour. They have translucent flesh that firms and turns opaque when cooked. While the shell of a live marron can vary from greenish black to electric blue, its colourful transition to bright orange when cooked is magical to watch.

The way to do justice to live seafood is by handling it with respect, killing it just prior to eating it and grilling it perfectly. When you source live seafood and kill it yourself, not only do you have a greater appreciation of the animal, but it tastes better as a result, too.

We opened Firedoor with this dish and it instantly became a firm favourite, capturing my philosophy of native ingredients speaking for themselves through the medium of fire. At the restaurant, we encourage our guests to appreciate the whole marron, including the sweet flesh from the claws as well as the succulent tail, and to combine these with the brain, coral, liver and the juices, which set to form a creamy custard. These elements combine well with the salty succulence of the native beach herbs and the fresh citrus pop of the finger lime.

1. Prepare your embers.

2. Kill the live marron using the ike-jime method (see Note) and split lengthways on a tray to catch the juices. Carefully remove the intestinal tract and discard.

3. Arrange a grill approximately 15 cm (6 in) above the embers.

4. Place the marron on the grill, shell side down, and pour the juices back into the head cavity. Season with sea salt.

5. Grill for approximately 3–4 minutes, at which point the delicate translucent flesh will turn opaque and the shell bright orange. The juices in the head should begin to set, forming a delicate custard.

6. Meanwhile, grill the finger limes for 1 minute, to release their essential oils. Split the finger limes lengthways and gently squeeze them between your finger and thumb to remove the vesicles.

7. In a small saucepan, warm the olive oil. Remove the marron from the grill and drizzle with the olive oil. Place the grilled finger lime vesicles in the head cavity of the marron.

8. Garnish with the beach herbs and serve immediately.

RECIPE TYPE *savoury*

WOOD TYPE
stone fruit, such as nectarine, peach or apricot

HEAT
medium-gentle embers

ADDITIONAL EQUIPMENT
grill

INGREDIENTS

4 live marron (see Note)

sea salt

4 finger limes (if out of season, use blood limes)

60 ml (2 fl oz/¼ cup) fruity, mild extra-virgin olive oil, such as arbequina or koroneiki, warmed

200 g (7 oz) mixed beach herbs, such as barilla and seablite

NOTES

Live marron, like all live crustaceans, deteriorate rapidly and should be consumed as soon as possible after purchase. Place in a covered, well-ventilated container lined with a damp cloth and keep in a cool place (between 6–16°C/40–60°F).

To kill humanely, chill the marron to 1°C (35°F) either in a refrigerator or by placing them in a freezer for 10 minutes. This renders them insensible. Execute the marron using the ike-jime method: swiftly insert the point of a sharp knife in the middle of the head, which is naturally indicated by a cross.

Baby squid
pickled celery, ink sauce

SERVES 4

Baby (loligo) squid is all too often used for bait rather than eating. It is typically line caught on a jigger, and has a beautiful balance of flavour and texture that is often lacking in larger species.

When cooking baby squid, it is important to keep the skin intact. It is covered in chromatophores, which give squid the ability to change colour and adapt to its environment. As well as protecting the squid from predators, this pigmented layer protects the delicate protein from the intense heat of the embers, retaining the squid's intrinsic flavour as it caramelises on the grill to reveal its rich reddish hue. In this dish, the buttermilk dressing adds a fresh acidity to the sweet crunch of the celery. It also makes good use of leftover buttermilk if you have made the Smoked butter on page 227.

1. Prepare your embers and arrange a grill cooling rack directly over the top.

2. Clean the squid, being careful not to tear the skin. Remove the ink sac, cartilage, eyes and beak. Rinse the body and tentacles, and reserve.

3. Prepare the celery salt. Remove the leaves from the celery, reserving 16 leaves to serve. Chop the remaining leaves in a food processor with the sea salt until fine. Spread evenly on a tray and leave to dry for 40 minutes. Once dry, grind in a mortar and pestle to an even consistency.

4. Peel the celery stalks to form long, thin strips. Place in a bowl of ice water to curl and crisp.

5. Prepare the squid ink sauce. Blend all the ingredients to a smooth cream using a hand blender. Pass through a fine-mesh sieve, season with sea salt to taste, and reserve.

6. Prepare the buttermilk dressing. Combine 50 ml (1¾ fl oz) of the buttermilk with the garlic and lemon zest in a bowl. Whisk in the olive oil.

7. Remove the celery strips from the ice water, toss them with the buttermilk dressing and season with the celery salt.

8. Grill the squid over the embers for 1–2 minutes on each side, turning once. Season with sea salt and remove from the grill. Place on a clean tray.

9. In a small saucepan, warm the olive oil, then pour it over the squid. Add the remaining buttermilk and strain all juices and the oil back into the pan. Bring back up to the heat, whisking continuously to allow a light emulsion to form.

10. Serve immediately in warmed bowls, with the squid placed atop the squid ink sauce. Finish with celery strips, pour over the combined juices and serve with the fresh almonds and celery leaves.

RECIPE TYPE *savoury*

WOOD TYPE
cherry

HEAT
intense embers

ADDITIONAL EQUIPMENT
grill cooling rack

INGREDIENTS

8 medium baby (loligo) squid

1 head celery, with leaves

20 g (¾ oz) sea salt, plus extra to season

50 ml (1¾ fl oz) fruity, mild extra-virgin olive oil, such as arbequina or koroneiki

100 g (3½ oz) fresh green almonds, peeled and halved

For the squid ink sauce

100 g (3½ oz/⅔ cup) raw almonds

½ slice grilled sourdough bread

100 ml (3½ fl oz) Tomato water (page 240)

15 g (½ oz) squid ink

½ garlic clove, blanched until soft

2 teaspoons cava vinegar

25 ml (¾ fl oz) fruity, mild extra-virgin olive oil, such as arbequina or koroneiki

sea salt

For the buttermilk dressing

100 ml (3½ fl oz) buttermilk (page 227)

½ garlic clove, blanched and minced

zest of ½ lemon

25 ml (¾ fl oz) fruity, mild extra-virgin olive oil, such as arbequina or koroneiki

Oysters
pickled kohlrabi, apple, sea lettuce

SERVES 4

Many people are surprised when any delicate ingredient, such as an oyster, is grilled. But it highlights one of the many advantages of grilling over real wood. The smoky, subtle perfume of a fruit wood, such as apple, marries well with the sweet, creamy brininess of pacific oysters, which benefit from being barely cooked.

1. Prepare your embers and arrange a grill approximately 15 cm (6 in) above the embers.

2. Prepare the oysters. Hold the oyster firmly in your hand with a cloth. With an oyster knife, dig gradually and firmly into one side of the oyster with a burrowing motion. When you feel the knife penetrate the shell, slide the knife beneath the top shell, severing the adductor muscle to open the oyster. Carefully remove the oyster from its shell, retaining all the juices. Clean and reserve the shells for serving. Using scissors, trim away the adductor muscle and the mantle. Strain the oyster juices through a fine-mesh sieve set over a bowl and reserve.

3. In a bowl, whisk together the vinegar, mirin and sea salt until the salt dissolves.

4. Peel the kohlrabi and slice (preferably using a mandolin) into 2 cm (¾ in) ribbons. Add to the vinegar mixture and leave to pickle for 10 minutes.

5. Peel and core the apple and cut into batons. Drain the pickled kohlrabi and mix in a bowl with the apple.

6. Place the oysters in the fine-mesh sieve and spray with grapeseed oil. Grill over gentle embers for 2 minutes on each side.

7. Place the sea lettuce over the grill to warm, then place in the bottom of the reserved oyster shells, followed by ribbons of pickled kohlrabi and apple batons.

8. Pour the reserved oyster juices into a saucepan and, over medium heat, bring to the boil. Whisk vigorously with 1 tablespoon of grapeseed oil until a foamy emulsion forms.

9. Place each oyster back in its shell, pour over the emulsified juices, top with the sea grapes and serve immediately.

RECIPE TYPE *savoury*

WOOD TYPE
apple

HEAT
gentle embers

ADDITIONAL EQUIPMENT
grill

INGREDIENTS

8 large pacific oysters

100 ml (3½ fl oz) rice vinegar

50 ml (1¾ fl oz) mirin

1 tablespoon sea salt

1 small kohlrabi

1 granny smith apple

1 tablespoon grapeseed oil, plus extra to spray

100 g (3½ oz) sea lettuce, soaked, rinsed and drained

100 g (3½ oz) sea grapes

School prawns
chilli, saltbush

SERVES 4

School prawns are one of the most delicious crustaceans, as they are the sweetest of all the prawns. At Firedoor we source prawns from just one fisherman who fishes a particular stretch of the Clarence River – and for some reason his prawns always taste better. Due to their small size, they are delicate and deteriorate rapidly, so must be super fresh off the boat. Often seen fried, the prawns taste even better off the grill and are best eaten with your fingers, crispy shell, legs and all. While you might find the idea of eating the shells texturally confronting, I urge you to give it a go.

1. Prepare your embers.

2. Prepare the prawns. Rinse them, removing any weeds or small fish that may be in the catch. Carefully remove the heads from the prawns, leaving the legs attached to the tail. Reserve the heads for the oil.

3. Prepare the aromatic oil. Heat 50 ml (1¾ fl oz) of the olive oil in a cast-iron pan and roast the coriander seeds, chilli seeds, ginger and garlic over the open fire or in a wood oven for 1 minute until fragrant. Add the reserved prawn heads, crushing them with the back of a large spoon to release more flavour. Continue to roast over a high heat (the prawn heads will turn bright orange) until all the water has evaporated. Add the remaining olive oil and orange zest, and heat to 70°C (160°F). Simmer for 20 minutes. Cool slightly, then pass through a fine-mesh sieve. Reserve.

4. Spray the prawns sparingly with grapeseed oil and grill in a fine-mesh sieve directly on top of the hot embers for 4–5 minutes, tossing regularly until the prawns turn a pinkish hue.

5. Season with sea salt, add the garlic chives to the prawns and grill for a further 30 seconds. Transfer the prawns to a clean bowl.

6. In a small cast-iron pan, heat the aromatic oil. Add the chilli and the saltbush leaves and fry until crisp. Pour the chilli oil over the grilled prawns.

7. Toss the prawns with the lemon zest and juice, and serve immediately.

RECIPE TYPE *savoury*

WOOD TYPE
orange

HEAT
medium-intense embers

ADDITIONAL EQUIPMENT
cast-iron pan, sugar thermometer

INGREDIENTS

500 g (1 lb 2 oz) fresh school prawns (shrimp)

250 ml (8½ fl oz/1 cup) extra-virgin olive oil

½ teaspoon coriander seeds

1 chilli, deseeded and finely sliced (reserve the seeds for the oil)

5 g (¼ oz) ginger root, finely minced

1 garlic clove, finely minced

zest of 1 orange

grapeseed oil, for spraying

sea salt

1 bunch flowering garlic chives

40 g (1½ oz) saltbush leaves

zest and juice of 1 lemon

Pipis
garlic, karkalla

SERVES 4

Found all along the eastern coast of Australia, pipis have long been an important food source for Indigenous Australians, found in many middens dating back more than 2000 years. I would take great delight in pipi-ing for fishing bait as a youngster, by shuffling in the sand between tides until I felt a shell pop between my toes. While you couldn't get fresher pipis, they were as gritty as hell. You have to ensure that pipis are well purged of sand prior to cooking. There is nothing worse than grit in your pipi.

1. Prepare your embers. Spread the embers evenly across the base of the grate and set a grill cooling rack 2½ cm (1 in) above the embers.

2. Place the pipis directly on the rack. Immediately cover with a lid and allow to cook for 2–3 minutes, or until they open.

3. Meanwhile, grill the garlic scapes and karkalla over the embers.

4. Uncover the pipis and, using a pair of tongs, carefully remove the pipis as they pop open, placing them into a clean bowl and retaining as much of the liquor as possible. Add the lemon zest and juice to the bowl.

5. In a small cast-iron pan, heat the olive oil. Add the chilli and gently fry until lightly golden. Pour the chilli oil over the pipis.

6. Strain the mix of oil, lemon and pipi juice into a warm saucepan and whisk to emulsify. Add the parsley and mix well.

7. Arrange the pipis in a bowl and pour the emulsified juices over, garnish with the garlic scapes and karkalla, and serve immediately.

RECIPE TYPE *savoury*

WOOD TYPE
apple

HEAT
intense embers

ADDITIONAL EQUIPMENT
grill cooling rack, lid, cast-iron pan

INGREDIENTS

1.6 kg (3½ lb) live pipis (or clams/vongoles), purged and cleaned (see Note)

1 bunch garlic scapes

100 g (3½ oz) karkalla (beach bananas), washed and picked

zest and juice of 1 lemon

100 ml (3½ fl oz) fruity, mild extra-virgin olive oil, such as arbequina or koroneiki

1 red chilli, deseeded and finely sliced

20 g (¾ oz) flat-leaf (Italian) parsley, finely chopped

NOTE

To prepare pipis, discard any that are chipped, broken, or damaged in any way. Tap to check that the shells are tightly closed, discarding any that remain open. Soak in salted water for 30 minutes to purge any remaining impurities. Remove the pipis and rinse in fresh water prior to cooking.

Red mullet
escabeche

SERVES 4

Incorrectly classed in the UK as mullet, red mullet is actually a member of the goatfish family and a favoured part of the Mediterranean diet. I worked with red mullet for years in Europe and it was only when I came to Australia, where they are often sold under the Greek nomenclature *barbounia*, that I realised the fish was not a true mullet. They were so valued in ancient Rome that they sold for their weight in silver. Though small, red mullet has a sweet and delicately flavoured flesh, and fine oil running under the skin that crisps up beautifully on the grill.

In this recipe, the escabeche refers to the pickled vegetables; the acidity completes the cooking of the mullet as it comes off the grill. The vibrant combination provides a taste of sunshine no matter what the weather.

1. Prepare your embers.

2. Scale and gut the fish, and remove the gills. Rinse quickly and dry well.

3. Butterfly the fish. Use a sharp knife to make an incision along the skin on the back of the fish to one side of the dorsal fin. Following this line, run the knife horizontally from the head to the tail, going halfway to the backbone. Move the knife through to the underside of the fish, then run the knife along the whole fillet. Turn the fish over and repeat on the other side.

4. With a pair of scissors, carefully cut the backbone free behind the head and in front of the tail. This will enable you to easily remove the backbone while retaining the head and tail, which hold the fish together during grilling.

5. Trim the belly. Locate the bones running along the middle of the top half of the fillet and carefully remove them using tweezers.

6. Prepare the escabeche vegetables. In a small saucepan, combine the zest and juice of the oranges and limes, the lemongrass and the fennel seeds. Bring to the boil and simmer until reduced to approximately 200 ml (7 fl oz) of liquid. Pass through a fine-mesh sieve and, while warm, pour over the sliced carrots and fennel. Leave for 40 minutes to macerate.

7. Season the flesh of the fish with sea salt, and grill in an enclosed grill rack over intense embers for 2 minutes, skin side down, until beautifully caramelised.

8. Meanwhile, drain the carrot and fennel (reserving the liquid) and grill for 2 minutes with the spring onions until lightly charred. Season, drizzle with olive oil and garnish with half of the fresh fennel fronds.

9. Transfer the fish to a clean tray, add the reserved escabeche liquid and allow to rest for 1 minute, during which time the acidity will finish cooking the fish.

10. Gently heat the olive oil in a small saucepan and pour it over the red mullet. Strain all the liquid back into the saucepan, whisking continuously and allowing a light emulsion to form.

11. Place the pickled and grilled vegetables on a plate, top with the fish and pour the emulsion over. Finish with the remaining fresh fennel fronds and the flowers. Serve immediately.

RECIPE TYPE *savoury*

WOOD TYPE
orange

HEAT
intense embers

ADDITIONAL EQUIPMENT
enclosed grill rack

INGREDIENTS

8 red mullet

zest and juice of 8 oranges

zest and juice of 2 limes

1 lemongrass stem, bruised and chopped finely

½ teaspoon fennel seeds

1 bunch baby carrots, peeled and finely sliced

3 baby fennel bulbs, outer layers peeled and finely sliced

sea salt

4 spring onions (scallions), finely chopped

100 ml (3½ fl oz) olive oil, plus extra to drizzle

½ bunch fennel fronds, picked

1 head fennel flowers

Scallops
lemon curd, dulse

SERVES 4

The beauty of cooking scallops on the fire is that you don't even need a pan – just place the shells directly on the embers. The shells transmit heat like a *plancha* (flat grill), caramelising on one side while the other remains barely cooked with a slight jelly-like texture that combines well with the richness of the grilled lemon curd. The spring onion keeps flavours on the savoury side, while the smoky dulse gives everything a salty umami kick.

1. Prepare your embers, burning a small fire. Place a grill cooling rack directly on top.

2. Prepare the grilled lemon curd. On the grill cooling rack, grill the whole lemons over the embers for 2 minutes until they are toasted and the essential oils release. Remove, zest and halve the lemons. Grill the lemon halves for 3 minutes, cut side down, until lightly caramelised. Remove and juice the lemons, adding the juice to the zest. In a small saucepan, whisk the eggs and the sugar. Add the lemon juice and zest, and the smoked butter. Continue whisking over a low heat for 8-10 minutes until the mixture is slightly thickened. Transfer to a clean container.

3. Prepare the scallops. With a small, flat knife, carefully prise open each scallop just wide enough to run the knife along the inside of the flat shell to release the adductor muscle. Using a spoon, remove the scallop from the curved shell, retaining the shells. Remove the mantle and gut, leaving the orange (occasionally purple) roe. Pat dry with paper towel and refrigerate immediately.

4. Drain the dulse and reserve.

5. Place the shells directly on a bed of embers to preheat. Place a spoon of olive oil in each shell and, once smoking, place a scallop, large surface down, on each shell. Grill for 2 minutes until seared and caramelised.

6. Place the dulse on the uncooked side of the scallop and leave for 1 minute before turning. Add the spring onions.

7. Remove the scallop shells from the fire, season with salt and serve immediately with a spoonful of the grilled lemon curd.

RECIPE TYPE *savoury*

WOOD TYPE
citrus

HEAT
medium embers

ADDITIONAL EQUIPMENT
grill cooling rack

INGREDIENTS

12 live scallops, in their shells

10 g (¼ oz) dried dulse, soaked in cold filtered water for 1 hour

100 ml (3½ fl oz) robust, zesty extra-virgin olive oil, such as picual

4 spring onions (scallions), finely chopped

sea salt

For the grilled lemon curd

3 lemons

3 eggs

180 g (6½ oz) caster (superfine) sugar

120 g (4½ oz) Smoked butter (page 227)

Sardines
bull's horn pepper

SERVES 4

In the words of Spanish chef Ferran Adrià, 'A very good sardine is always preferable to a not-that-good lobster'. This is a reminder that an ingredient is only as valuable as its quality. Sadly sardines are too often cast aside (quite literally) as baitfish or viewed as something fishy and bony that comes in tins. A fresh sardine in rigor with its silver blue hue is a beauty to behold. Nobody in the world values the sardine more than the Portuguese, who take to the streets of the capital every year in celebration of their patron saint's day to grill thousands of the small fish.

Unlike their tinned cousins, grilled fresh sardines exude a delicate oiliness and a briny tang. In this recipe, they are brightened by the sweet vibrancy of the long, thin bull's horn peppers, which are blistered and blackened to remove their skins then slow roasted, intensifying their sweet flesh.

RECIPE TYPE	*savoury*

WOOD TYPE
orange

HEAT
intense embers

ADDITIONAL EQUIPMENT
grill, enclosed grill rack

INGREDIENTS

12 fresh sardines

10 bull's horn peppers

4 garlic cloves, sliced, trimmings retained for bread

½ bunch flat-leaf (Italian) parsley, leaves picked

2 sourdough slices

100 ml (3½ fl oz) fruity, mild extra-virgin olive oil, such as arbequina or koroneiki

sea salt

juice of ½ lemon

1. Prepare your embers. Arrange a grill approximately 10 cm (4 in) above the embers.

2. Scale and gut the fish, and remove the heads. Rinse quickly and dry well. Slide your thumbnail along and under the spine from the head to the tail. Press down gently on the spine to butterfly the fish, releasing the spine from the flesh before gently pulling it away. Trim the belly, removing the rib bones. Rinse briefly and pat dry well with paper towel.

3. Grill 8 of the peppers whole, turning frequently until blistered and blackened all over. Transfer to a bowl or tray, cover with a lid or cloth and allow to steam for 5-10 minutes.

4. Juice the remaining 2 peppers, then pass the juice through a sieve into a small saucepan. Boil over a medium heat until the liquid is reduced to a syrupy consistency. Set aside.

5. When they are cool enough to handle, carefully peel the blackened peppers, removing the seeds and retaining the grilled pepper juices. Add the grilled pepper juices to the reduced pepper juice and spoon it over the warm grilled peppers.

6. In a saucepan of salted boiling water, blanch the garlic for 1 minute until tender, then drain and reserve. Repeat with the parsley, blanching for 2 minutes.

7. Rub the sourdough slices with 2 tablespoons of olive oil and the garlic trimmings, and grill until golden and toasted. Tear into small pieces and reserve.

8. Season the flesh of the fish with sea salt, then grill in an enclosed grill rack for 2 minutes, skin side down, until beautifully caramelised. Transfer to a clean tray.

9. In a small saucepan, heat the remaining olive oil and pour it over the sardines. Add the lemon juice and strain all the juices, along with the oil, back into the pan, whisking continuously until a light emulsion forms.

10. Arrange the sardines on top of the peppers on serving plates, followed by the blanched garlic and parsley. Finish by drizzling with the warm emulsion and scattering over the toasted sourdough. Serve immediately.

Prawns

How good can a prawn be? To this day, I still remember my first one at Etxebarri. I had been working there for a couple of weeks before an opportunity came to try one of the *gambas*, which came from the small fishing village of Palamos on the east coast of Spain. The deep coastal shelf off the east coast sees the prawns netted from depths of over 100 metres (328 feet). The sudden change in pressure when they are brought to the surface causes instant death.

They looked like amazing prawns, large, succulent and bright pink, but I didn't think anything more of them. I had eaten many prawns over the years and this was just one grilled prawn on a plate with nothing more than some sea salt ... its simple appearance was disarming. I placed the prawn in my mouth and sucked on the head. I was overwhelmed with a sudden wave of emotion; in one mouthful the prawn juices imparted the subtle smoke of the grill, the intense natural character of the prawn and the fresh, briny taste of the sea. It was so good, I cried.

Australia is famous for its prawns and has coined the phrase 'shrimp on the barbie' as part of its culinary culture, which speaks of the abundance of great seafood as much as the Aussie outdoor lifestyle. But Australia is a big country and prawns do not travel particularly well. Most prawns are either sold cooked, frozen and/or treated with sodium metabisulfite, which is a chemical the prawns are washed in to improve shelf life and prevent discolouration. While you may pay more for fresh, wild, untreated prawns, it is worthwhile, as prawns have a very delicate and creamy texture that can be readily ruined by poor handling.

1. Prepare your embers. Arrange a grill approximately 15 cm (6 in) above them.

2. Prepare the prawns. Using the point of a sharp knife, make a small incision at the base of the prawn, just above the tail on the inner side, releasing the base of the digestive tract. Locate the other end of the digestive tract between the body and head. Using small tweezers or the point of a sharp knife, carefully pull to remove the digestive tract and discard.

3. Spray the prawns sparingly with grapeseed oil and season with sea salt.

4. Grill the prawns for 2–3 minutes. The shell will turn from a light bluish grey to an orangey pink.

5. Carefully turn the prawns, spray again with grapeseed oil and season with sea salt. Grill for a further 2–3 minutes. The shells should be lightly toasted from the grill, not charred, and have a sweet aroma with no indication of ammonia. The meat inside the tail will have firmed up and turned opaque. The prawns are cooked when the juices in the heads begin to bubble gently.

6. Garnish with the seablite and serve immediately.

RECIPE TYPE *savoury*

WOOD TYPE
orange

HEAT
medium embers

ADDITIONAL EQUIPMENT
grill

INGREDIENTS

8 wild raw prawns (shrimp) (see Note)

grapeseed oil, for spraying

sea salt

16 seablite sprigs

NOTE

Source fresh, wild untreated prawns. If you want to prepare them and grill them later, you are best to keep them in an iced 5% salt brine solution (page 240) where they will keep for up to 36 hours.

Mussels éclade
fennel and saffron rouille

SERVES 4

The name *éclade* is thought to be a derivative of *aiguillade* (from the French *aiguille*: needle), referring to the hundreds of dried pine needles used to cook the mussels for this dish. Pine needles burn intensely for a brief period, just long enough to cook the mussels while infusing them with a smoky woody sweetness.

For this dish it is important that the mussels are positioned vertically on a board, hinge upwards. Four nails are often hammered halfway into the centre of a board as a supporting structure. The mussels are then tightly arranged against each other, and spiralling out from the centre, to stop them opening when cooking. While the careful arrangement of mussels may be an involved process, the pyrotechnic spectacle is almost as satisfying as eating them.

This is finger food at its best, served with a fennel and saffron rouille into which each mussel is dipped as it is picked from the shell.

1. To arrange the mussels on your board, start in the centre using the nails as props. Position each mussel so that its shell hinge is facing upwards. This is so that the mussels do not fill with ash as they cook.

2. Pile the pine needles on top of the mussels, ensuring that the mussels are completely covered to a depth of at least 20 cm (8 in).

3. Prepare the rouille. In a saucepan, bring the milk and saffron to the boil, then remove from the heat. Pass the potato and garlic through a fine sieve and place in a food processor with the egg yolks. Blend, gradually adding the olive oil in a steady stream. Add the warm saffron milk, check the seasoning and strain through a fine-mesh sieve. Add the chopped fennel fronds and the lemon juice and zest and combine well.

4. When you are ready to eat, set light to the pine needles and stand back, as they will catch and burn with an intense flame. The fire will eventually run out of fuel and the flames will extinguish themselves, leaving the mussels with a light covering of ash.

5. The shells will be hot, so allow them to cool slightly before handling. Allow guests to prise the mussels from their shells, dip in the rouille and devour.

RECIPE TYPE *savoury*

WOOD TYPE
dried pine needles

HEAT
intense flame

ADDITIONAL EQUIPMENT
wooden board with 4 nails positioned in a square formation 2 cm (¾ in) apart in the centre

INGREDIENTS
2 kg (4 lb 6 oz) live mussels, cleaned (see Note)

For the fennel and saffron rouille
100 ml (3½ fl oz) milk

1 x 1 g (0.03 oz) packet saffron threads

60 g (2 oz) cooked potato flesh

1 garlic clove, finely minced

2 egg yolks

180 ml (6 fl oz) fruity, mild extra-virgin olive oil, such as arbequina or koroneiki

sea salt

½ bunch fennel fronds, finely chopped

zest and juice of ½ lemon

NOTE

To prepare the mussels, discard any that are chipped, broken or damaged in any way. Tap to check that the mussels are tightly closed, discarding any that are open.

If necessary, remove the beard (or byssus thread), which is what attached the mussel to the rope or rock it grew on, and scrub clean. Soak in salted water for 30 minutes to purge any remaining impurities. Remove the mussels and rinse in fresh water before cooking.

Blue swimmer crab
rye bread, lime crème fraîche

SERVES 4

Of all the shellfish, for me crab would ultimately have to be the most satisfying, as it requires greater effort and a certain determination to prise the sweet goodness from its shell. Nowadays we tend to eat too quickly, with more time spent cooking than eating. With crab the reverse is true, as the speed and simplicity of the cooking enables us to spend more time savouring the experience of eating. With their clean taste and firm texture, blue swimmer crabs are delicious and require little more accompaniment than some dark rye bread, a little crème fraîche and a good bottle of wine.

1. Prepare your embers and place a grill approximately 20 cm (8 in) above them.

2. Place each whole crab, carapace side down, directly on the grill and cover with a metal bowl or tray. Cook for 8 minutes, turn the crabs over, spray generously with oil, then cook for a further 3 minutes. The crab is done when the juices start to bubble between the front claw and body joint. Remove and allow to cool enough to handle.

3. One by one, place a crab in a clean dish, and turn onto its back. Carefully place your thumbs in between the flap and the carapace, then press with your thumbs to pop open the carapace. Pull away the grey gills, or 'dead man's fingers', and discard. With a sharp, heavy knife, split the crab in half. Break the body into smaller sections while removing the tasty white meat. Reserve.

4. In a bowl, combine the crème fraîche with the dill and lime zest and juice. Season with sea salt and pepper.

5. Spread the crème fraîche over the bread, and top with crabmeat and a squeeze of lime juice. Serve garnished with dill fronds.

RECIPE TYPE *savoury*

WOOD TYPE
apple

HEAT
medium-intense embers

ADDITIONAL EQUIPMENT
grill, metal bowl or tray

INGREDIENTS

4 × 500 g (1 lb 2 oz) blue swimmer crabs (1 crab per person), yielding approximately 100 g (3½ oz) meat from each crab (see Note)

grapeseed oil, for spraying

400 g (14 oz) crème fraîche

1 tablespoon chopped dill, plus extra to garnish

zest and juice of 1 lime, plus extra to squeeze

sea salt and black pepper

8 slices of Black bread (page 235) or good-quality rye bread

NOTE

When buying crabs, remember they should feel heavy for their size and have their legs and claws intact.

Caviar

Caviar, I hear you cry! Why would we take such a fine ingredient and subject it to the primitive grill? It sounds crazy, I know, but perhaps more than any other ingredient, caviar highlights the boundless potential of cooking over a wood fire. I first grilled caviar at Etxebarri and it was one of the greatest challenges of my time there. It took almost a year until we were happy with the result (for the full story, see page 17). It was also one of the few occasions that the idea came before the ingredient, as caviar was not local to the Basque country. Although we tried serving it with various accompaniments, from grilled crab blood custard to tiger milk (otherwise known as *chufa*) and even snail caviar, we felt it spoke loudest and clearest just on its own.

1. Prepare your embers.

2. Carefully place the caviar on a fine-mesh sieve or mesh pan, spreading it to form a layer about 1 cm (½ in) thick.

3. Lay the seaweed strands over the burning embers, which will emanate steam and smoke.

4. Suspend the fine-mesh sieve or mesh pan with the caviar 30 cm (12 in) above the embers, and cover with a glass lid.

5. Grill for 3–4 minutes, heating the caviar to blood temperature: you will notice the fat beginning to separate the individual eggs, and the eggs taking on a glossy appearance.

6. Divide between 4 spoons and serve immediately. To eat, place the entire amount in the mouth at once.

RECIPE TYPE *savoury*
WOOD TYPE *apple*
HEAT *gentle embers*
ADDITIONAL EQUIPMENT *glass lid*

INGREDIENTS

60 g (2 oz) unsalted beluga imperial 000 caviar (see Note)

1 large handful fresh seaweed

NOTE

Caviar is a delicacy that can deteriorate rapidly. It should be consumed as soon as possible after purchase. Keep it in the coolest part of the refrigerator.

SEAFOOD

Otoro tuna
fennel, edamame

SERVES 4

Otoro is the most prized part of tuna, as it comes from the lowest section of the belly (*otoro*) where there is the highest concentration of fat. The natural fats that run through otoro are rich with omega-3 oils, making it well suited for grilling. Ideally it should be served warm and rare so that it melts in your mouth. In this dish, otoro's soft richness is contrasted by the slightly sweet crunch of aromatic fennel. The fresh zing of grilled finger limes complete the dish.

1. Prepare your embers.

2. Trim and peel the tough fibres from the fennel, then slice it thinly using a mandoline. Reserve the fine fronds.

3. Grill the edamame for 2–3 minutes until lightly charred. Remove and allow to cool enough to handle, then pod the beans.

4. Lightly season the tuna belly and grill in the enclosed grill rack for 3 minutes on each side. Transfer to a clean tray.

5. Grill the finger limes for 1 minute, just to release their essential oils. Split the finger limes lengthways and gently squeeze them between your finger and thumb to remove the vesicles.

6. In a bowl, dress the fennel slices with the olive oil, the lime zest and juice and the fennel fronds. Season to taste. Toss through the edamame.

7. Slice the tuna belly across the grain using a sharp knife. Divide the fennel salad and sliced tuna belly between serving plates. Scatter with the finger lime vesicles and serve immediately.

RECIPE TYPE *savoury*

WOOD TYPE
apple

HEAT
gentle embers

ADDITIONAL EQUIPMENT
enclosed grill rack

INGREDIENTS

1 fennel bulb

200 g (7 oz) edamame

sea salt

600 g (1 lb 5 oz) tuna belly

4 finger limes

50 ml (1¾ fl oz) fruity, mild extra-virgin olive oil, such as arbequina or koroneiki

zest and juice of ½ lime

Mackerel
bagnet vert, watermelon radish

SERVES 4

A wonderful oily fish, blue or slimy mackerel is often overlooked as it is regarded as a baitfish and spoils readily. But its high natural oil content makes for perfect grilling, as the skin caramelises beautifully over the dry intense heat of the embers. Here it is grilled with hay, which contains coumarin, a sweet-smelling organic chemical compound that cuts the fattiness of the fish with a vanilla flavour. The vibrant pepperiness of the *bagnet vert* (Italian green salsa), the vinegar in the pickle and the fresh heat of the horseradish provide a simple yet effective accompaniment.

1. Prepare your embers.

2. Scale and gut the fish, and remove the gills. Rinse quickly and dry well.

3. With a sharp knife, fillet the mackerel, leaving the skin on. Place the fillet skin side down and locate the bones running along the middle of the fillet. With a sharp knife, cut either side of the bones to form a 'V'. Carefully lift out and discard the V-shaped strip of flesh containing the pin bones. (Also see Note.)

4. Prepare the bagnet vert. Wash the parsley and rocket in ice water to refresh them, before draining to remove any excess water. Soak the bread in the filtered water for 20 minutes. Squeeze the bread to remove excess water and purée in a food processor with the olive oil and vinegar until a smooth cream forms. Add the capers and anchovies, and blend on high speed. Check the seasoning and store in the refrigerator until needed.

5. Using a mandoline, thinly slice the watermelon radish, season with sea salt, then place in a bowl with the vinegar for 20 minutes.

6. Lay the fish in the enclosed grill rack, skin side down. Season with sea salt and grill over intense embers until the skin bubbles and crisps.

7. Remove the fish from the embers and throw the damp hay onto the embers.

8. Hold the fish, skin side up, just above the smoking hay for 30 seconds. Season the fish with sea salt and transfer to a clean tray.

9. In a small saucepan, gently warm the olive oil and pour it over the mackerel. Sprinkle with the vinegar from the pickled radish and strain all the juices, along with the oil, back into the pan, whisking continuously until a light emulsion has formed.

10. Arrange the fish on a plate. Serve the mackerel alongside the bagnet vert with slices of pickled watermelon radish and grated horseradish.

RECIPE TYPE *savoury*

WOOD TYPE
olive, handful of hay soaked in water for 20 minutes and drained

HEAT
intense embers

ADDITIONAL EQUIPMENT
enclosed grill rack

INGREDIENTS

2 slimy or blue mackerel, cleaned (see Note)

2 watermelon radishes

sea salt

40 ml (1¼ fl oz) cava vinegar

100 ml (3½ fl oz) robust, zesty extra-virgin olive oil, such as picual

10 g (¼ oz) fresh horseradish root, grated

For the bagnet vert

60 g (2 oz) flat-leaf (Italian) parsley, leaves picked

60 g (2 oz) rocket (arugula) leaves

1 slice fresh bread, crust removed

100 ml (3½ fl oz) filtered water

150 ml (5 fl oz) fruity, mild extra-virgin olive oil, such as arbequina or koroneiki

1 tablespoon red-wine vinegar

1 tablespoon capers

2 anchovies in oil

sea salt

NOTE

You can buy mackerel already filleted if you prefer.

Abalone
black bean, beach herbs

SERVES 4

A member of the gastropod family, abalone has a single shell and a large adductor muscle that clings tenaciously to its rocky habitat, where it is well camouflaged. Limited harvesting, which is difficult and dangerous, means that it commands a high price. It is known as *pāua* in New Zealand, where it forms a strong part of the Māori culture and traditional diet, and is revered as a treasure. My first experience of abalone was being invited to a local *hangi* in Kaikoura, New Zealand, where most of the food was cooked slowly in a giant earth oven. I remember it was rich, smoky and delicious – food for the soul as much as for the stomach. I had never come across it in Europe and was keen to work with it in Australia. Being a muscle, it has a firm texture and is often sliced thinly and eaten raw, or cooked slowly until it softens. Abalone must be tenderised before grilling to make it palatable. The Māori understand this, often beating it with a rock until tender before placing it on the fire. In this dish, the texture is firm but yielding and there is an almost buttery richness that pairs well with the intense salty-savoury umami of the black bean.

1. Prepare your embers.

2. Prepare the black bean sauce. Soak the black beans in water for 1 hour. Rinse, drain and reserve.

3. Heat the oil in a small saucepan over a medium-high heat. Add the garlic, ginger and chilli, and cook for 2 minutes until softened and fragrant. Add the spring onion and the drained black beans, cook for a further 1 minute, then add the remaining ingredients. Bring to the boil. Reduce the heat to medium and simmer, uncovered, for 10-12 minutes or until the liquid is reduced by half.

4. Prepare the abalone. Remove each one from its shell using a large spoon, sliding the spoon around the edge between the flesh and the shell, and scooping the top of the foot loose from its attachment to the shell. Using a sharp knife, remove the intestine from the underside. Cut off the small piece of gristle where the muscle was attached to the shell. Continue cutting around the foot on both sides, removing the mantle. Cut a thin layer off the base of the foot where it attached to the rock, trimming the entire surface of the dark exterior mantle and scraping off any brown film. Rinse well in cold water and dry on paper towel.

5. Place the abalone in a clean cloth and beat evenly with a tenderising hammer, heavy-based saucepan or a flat rock until pliable. Leave to rest for at least 10 minutes.

6. Arrange a grill cooling rack directly on the embers.

7. Repeat the tenderising process for the abalone, then place directly on the grill cooling rack and grill for 2-3 minutes on each side, seasoning both sides with sea salt. Remove from the grill, brush each abalone with the black bean sauce and allow to rest for 1 minute. Slice thinly.

8. Meanwhile, grill the herbs in a fine-mesh sieve for 1 minute over the embers.

9. Carefully place the sliced abalone back in their shells and spoon over the remaining black bean sauce. Finish by topping with the grilled beach herbs and serve immediately.

RECIPE TYPE *savoury*

WOOD TYPE
apple

HEAT
intense embers

ADDITIONAL EQUIPMENT
grill cooling rack

INGREDIENTS

4 abalone (see Note)

sea salt

beach herbs, such as karkalla, seablite and warrigal greens

For the black bean sauce

50 g (1¾ oz) fermented black beans (douchi)

1 tablespoon sesame oil

1 tablespoon finely minced garlic

1 tablespoon finely minced ginger

½ red chilli, deseeded and finely chopped

1 spring onion (scallion), finely chopped

60 ml (2 fl oz/¼ cup) chicken stock

2 teaspoons shaoxing rice wine

1 tablespoon soy sauce

1 teaspoon sugar

½ teaspoon rice vinegar

1 tablespoon toasted black sesame seeds

NOTES

Live abalone, like all live crustaceans, deteriorate rapidly and should be eaten as soon as possible.

Place in a well-ventilated container covered with a wet, heavy cloth and keep in a cool place (between 6-16°C/40-60°F) for up to 3 days.

Flathead
kale, radishes

SERVES 4

Flathead is one of Australia's most iconic and versatile fish and is a staple for fish and chips due to its white colour and firm, flaky texture. Although the batter protects it, cooking it this way, as a fillet, does not carry the benefits of grilling it on the bone. The grill radiates heat through the skeletal structure to release the pockets of gelatine found along the spinal column, resulting in soft and unctuous flesh.

1. Prepare your embers.

2. Scale and gut the fish, and remove the gills. Rinse quickly and dry well.

3. With a sharp pair of scissors, remove the dorsal and anal fins, retaining both the pectoral and pelvic fins, which are the wings.

4. Season the cavity well and, in an enclosed grill rack, grill approximately 15 cm (6 in) above evenly distributed embers for 12-15 minutes, turning halfway through cooking. The eyes should begin to pop, indicating that the fish is nearly cooked.

5. Transfer the fish to a clean tray, season well and leave in a warm place to rest and finish cooking. It should be easy to insert the blunt end of a spoon into the spine.

6. Meanwhile, arrange a grill cooling rack approximately 5 cm (2 in) above the embers. Spray the kale lightly with olive oil and grill for 2 minutes until crisp and lightly charred. Remove from the heat, season with sea salt, and shave the radishes over the top using a mandolin (the radishes will soften over the heat).

7. In a small pan, gently warm the remaining olive oil and pour it over the fish. Sprinkle with the vinegar and strain all the juices, along with the oil, back into the pan. Whisk continuously over a gentle heat until an emulsion has formed. Stir through the parsley.

8. Arrange the grilled kale and radishes on serving plates. Place the flathead on top, drizzle with the emulsion and serve immediately.

RECIPE TYPE *savoury*

WOOD TYPE
apple

HEAT
medium-intense embers

ADDITIONAL EQUIPMENT
enclosed grill rack, grill cooling rack

INGREDIENTS

1 flathead, approximately 800 g–1 kg (1 lb 12 oz–2 lb 3 oz), scaled and cleaned

sea salt

1 bunch kale, leaves picked and washed

150 ml (5 fl oz) extra-virgin olive oil, plus extra for spraying

1 bunch breakfast radishes

40 ml (1¼ fl oz) cava vinegar

1 handful flat-leaf (Italian) parsley, finely sliced

John Dory
cabbage, barilla

SERVES 4

John Dory is an amazing dense-textured fish with an incredible sweet and fatty flavour; its thin fillets are best cooked on the bone to retain maximum flavour and texture.

The name is said to derive from the French words *jaune d'or*, meaning golden yellow – which I like to believe, as its olive-yellow hue is often a good indicator of freshness. It is also known as Saint Peter's fish, the legend being that the patron saint of fishing taught fishermen how to pick up the fish without cutting their hands on the long sharp spine, by grabbing it just behind the gills. In picking it up, Saint Peter pressed his thumb and forefinger to the skin, creating its distinctive black spot. Given that John Dory has never swum in the Sea of Galilee, this is a much harder leap of faith. Either way, the fish uses its beauty spot to its advantage, scaring off predators when they approach, meaning there is all the more John Dory in the sea for us to enjoy.

In Spain we used to eat cabbage sautéed with garlic and chilli both as an accompaniment to fish and as a dish in its own right. Here the flavours are re-created on the grill, with the cabbage taking on an amazing sweetness, which complements the dory beautifully.

1. Prepare your embers.

2. Scale and gut the fish, and remove the gills and head. Rinse quickly and dry well.

3. Season the cavity of the fish with sea salt, then place the fish in an enclosed grill rack. Grill one side of the fish approximately 10 cm (4 in) above evenly distributed embers for 8-10 minutes.

4. Turn over the enclosed grill rack and grill the fish on the other side for a further 8-10 minutes, until beautifully caramelised.

5. Transfer the fish to a clean tray, season well with sea salt and allow to rest for 5 minutes.

6. Meanwhile, toss the cabbage and leek together in a bowl, then grill in a fine-mesh sieve until lightly charred and just cooked. Season and dress with lemon zest and juice, a drizzle of olive oil and chervil.

7. In a small saucepan, gently warm the olive oil and pour it over the fish. Put the vinegar into the pan and strain all the juices from the fish into the pan. Heat the liquid, whisking continuously, allowing an emulsion to form.

8. Arrange the grilled cabbage and leek on serving plates and place the fish on top. Pour the emulsion over, finish with the barilla and serve immediately.

RECIPE TYPE *savoury*

WOOD TYPE
apple

HEAT
intense embers

ADDITIONAL EQUIPMENT
enclosed grill rack

INGREDIENTS

1 whole John Dory, approximately 2 kg (4 lb 6 oz)

sea salt

1 baby spring cabbage, shredded finely

1 leek, tender part removed and cut into 5 mm (¼ in) dice

zest and juice of ½ lemon

200 ml (7 fl oz) robust, zesty extra-virgin olive oil, such as picual, plus extra to drizzle

½ bunch chervil, picked and finely chopped

50 ml (1¾ fl oz) cava vinegar

100 g (3½ oz) barilla (native spinach), picked and washed

Octopus
radicchio, macadamia

SERVES 4

Octopus can be a challenge to grill as all of its strength and muscle structure is distributed throughout its eight arms, making it quite firm and rubbery. Like its cephalopod cousin the squid, octopus is either best cooked very quickly or very slowly and should be tenderised before cooking – it is said that the Greeks would traditionally beat octopus forty times on a rock.

At the restaurant, we use a medium octopus from the Roaring Forties waters of the Bass Strait. They are captured using a specially designed pot and then tenderised. The intense heat of the embers cooks the octopus really quickly, maintaining its tenderness. Here, cooking over a wood fire imbues octopus with a smoky char, complemented by the bittersweet radicchio and enriched with buttery guanciale and the creamy texture of macadamia which, when finely shaved, looks like parmesan.

1. Prepare your embers and arrange a grill cooling rack directly on top.

2. Prepare the octopus. Remove the tentacles from the body, rinse under running water, and pat dry with a clean cloth.

3. Toss the radicchio with half of the olive oil and vinegar, and grill over the embers for 2 minutes on each side.

4. Grill the octopus over the embers for 2 minutes on each side, turning once. Season with sea salt and remove from the heat.

5. Dress the radicchio and octopus with the remaining olive oil and vinegar, and the orange zest.

6. Place the guanciale on a metal tray 20 cm (8 in) above the embers and gently warm until translucent.

7. Slice each tentacle into 4 pieces and place on a serving plate among the leaves of charred radicchio.

8. Finish with strips of warm guanciale, pour over the combined juices and scatter with the shaved macadamias and agretti sprigs.

RECIPE TYPE *savoury*

WOOD TYPE
preferably cherry

HEAT
intense embers

ADDITIONAL EQUIPMENT
grill cooling rack

INGREDIENTS

1 medium octopus, tenderised (see Notes)

1 head radicchio treviso, quartered (see Notes)

60 ml (2 fl oz/¼ cup) extra-virgin olive oil

20 ml (¾ fl oz) aged red-wine vinegar

sea salt

zest of ½ orange

12 wafer-thin slices guanciale (cured pork jowl)

100 g (3½ oz) fresh macadamias, preferably shaved finely on a mandoline

12 agretti sprigs

NOTES

Feel the tentacles to assess tenderness – they should feel limp, not rubbery.

Radicchio treviso has a less bitter profile than normal radicchio. If using normal radicchio, you may wish to use a sweeter vinegar, such as Pedro Ximénez vinegar, instead of aged red-wine vinegar.

Salt-crusted snapper
potatoes

SERVES 4

Cooking in a salt crust encases and protects ingredients from the extreme heat of the fire. I first experienced this method in a restaurant in Spain, where the dish made quite a dramatic entrance; the fish was served whole and the crust was broken open at the table. Inside there lay the most beautiful sea bass trapped within the hardened salt, which had formed the perfect oven. The flesh inside was rich and moist and, in spite of the incredible amount of salt, perfectly seasoned. The insulation of the salt enables the fish to retain all its flavour and juices while it is gently smoked from the wood fire. The potatoes are placed around the fish and are a delight to discover – like hidden jewels among the baked salt. The wrinkly salted skins of the potatoes give way to the soft flesh within, and are delicious dipped in salsa verde (page 244).

1. Prepare your embers. Remove 100 g (3½ oz) of the ashes and allow to cool completely.

2. Scale and gut the fish, and remove the gills. Rinse quickly and dry well.

3. Prepare the salt crust. Combine the rock salt with the egg whites, reserved and cooled ashes, fennel seeds, fennel flowers, orange zest and water to form a paste with the consistency of damp sand.

4. On a large, flat, heavy steel baking tray, spread half of the salt mix to form a bed the same size and shape as the fish and approximately 1 cm (½ in) thick.

5. Stuff the cavity of the fish with the orange slices, bay leaves and fennel fronds, and place the fish on the bed of salt. Nestle the potatoes around the fish and cover with the remaining salt mix, ensuring that the fish and potatoes are well sealed top to tail.

6. Place on a bed of embers, raking the embers around the edges and on top of the salt-crusted fish to cover completely.

7. Leave to bake for 20–25 minutes, at which point the crust will have hardened.

8. Remove from the fire and allow to rest for 10 minutes.

9. Take to the table and crack open the salt crust. Carefully lift the crust, which should come away in one large piece. Peel off any skin remaining on the fish to expose the succulent flesh, which should separate easily from the bones. Serve with good olive oil and fresh lemon wedges.

RECIPE TYPE *savoury*

WOOD TYPE
orange/citrus

HEAT
medium embers

ADDITIONAL EQUIPMENT
steel baking tray, or wood-fired oven or infiernillo

INGREDIENTS

1 × 2 kg (4 lb 6 oz) snapper

2 bay leaves

½ bunch fennel fronds

400 g (14 oz) baby potatoes (mixed varieties)

100 ml (3½ fl oz) fruity, mild extra-virgin olive oil, such as arbequina or koroneiki

1 lemon, cut into wedges

For the salt crust

3 kg (6 lb 10 oz) rock salt

6 egg whites, lightly beaten

100 g (3½ oz) ashes from the fire

1 tablespoon fennel seeds

1 head fennel flowers

2 oranges, zested and sliced (reserve slices for fish cavity)

150 ml (5 fl oz) filtered water

ALTERNATIVE METHOD

The fish can also be baked in a wood-fired oven or infiernillo (as illustrated on page 56).

Murray cod
Jerusalem artichokes, rainbow chard

SERVES 4

Murray cod is somewhat of an enigma, as it is not a member of the cod family; it is Australia's largest native freshwater fish. It has a rich, succulent texture with a layer of sweet, creamy fat. In the restaurant we only use cod from one particular fishery, Uarah in Grong Grong, where Bruce Malcolm (affectionately known as 'The Codfather') is a pioneer in his field and produces a cod with a clean, sweet earthiness rather than the muddiness for which the fish can be known. Its high value and rich flavour mean that every bit should be used; some of the best-tasting parts are found in the wings and the cheeks. When grilled, the skin becomes crisp and glassy, like fish crackling, while the flesh remains moist and unctuous. Jerusalem artichoke has a clean earthiness that is the best marriage for the cod, as the outside caramelises to an incredible sweetness that perfectly complements the creamy interior.

1. Prepare your embers.

2. Prepare the fish, carefully scaling and gutting it. Rinse quickly and dry well.

3. Butterfly the fish. Use a sharp knife to make an incision along the skin on the back of the fish to one side of the dorsal fin. Following this line, run the knife horizontally from the head to the tail, going halfway to the backbone. Move the knife through to the underside of the fish, then run the knife along the whole fillet. Turn the fish over and repeat on the other side.

4. With a pair of scissors, carefully cut the backbone free behind the head and in front of the tail. This will enable you to easily remove the backbone while retaining the head and tail, which hold the fish together during grilling.

5. Trim the belly. Locate the bones running along the middle of the top half of the fillet and carefully remove them using tweezers.

6. Prepare the sweet-pickled stems. Wash the rainbow chard and separate the leaves from the stems. Peel the chard stems, removing any woody strands, and dice evenly. In a saucepan, bring the water, vinegar and sugar to the boil, stirring to dissolve the sugar. Add the diced chard stems. Remove from the heat and leave to pickle for at least 20 minutes.

7. Grill the Jerusalem artichokes whole in an enclosed grill rack for 15–20 minutes, turning continuously until charred all over and soft when gently squeezed.

8. Season the inside of the fish well and place in an enclosed grill rack. Grill 15 cm (6 in) above evenly distributed embers for 12 minutes, turning the cod during the last 4 minutes of cooking to set the protein. The eyes should begin to pop. Transfer the fish to a clean tray, season well with sea salt and leave in a warm place to rest.

9. Meanwhile, spray the rainbow chard leaves lightly with olive oil and grill over the embers for 2 minutes until slightly crisp and charred. Season. Drain the chard stems of the pickle and toss through the leaves. The colourful stems should appear as little jewels among the leaves.

10. In a small saucepan, gently heat the olive oil. Pour it over the fish, add the vinegar and strain all the juices and the oil back in to the pan, whisking continuously to form an emulsion.

11. Arrange the grilled chard on a serving plate with the fish on top, pour the emulsion over it and serve immediately with the roasted artichokes.

RECIPE TYPE *savoury*

WOOD TYPE
apple

HEAT
medium-intense embers

ADDITIONAL EQUIPMENT
enclosed grill rack

INGREDIENTS

1 Murray cod, approximately 1.6 kg (3½ oz)

1 bunch rainbow chard

400 g (14 oz) Jerusalem artichokes, scrubbed

sea salt

150 ml (5 fl oz) extra-virgin olive oil, plus extra for spraying

40 ml (1¼ fl oz) apple-cider vinegar

For the sweet pickle

50 ml (1¾ fl oz) filtered water

50 ml (1¾ fl oz) apple-cider vinegar

50 g (1¾ oz) sugar

Turbot

Anton Chekhov once wrote, 'I stuffed myself with bread so as not to dream of turbot', but no amount of bread can satiate my hunger for this fish. It is simply incredible and unmatched in its meaty goodness. Turbot is one of the most prized fish of the Atlantic coast and during my time in the Basque country we often cooked large specimens weighing up to 7 kilograms (15½ pounds). To really do justice to this fish and to truly understand it, you must cook it whole, preferably over a wood fire. I encourage you to savour every part of it, from the succulent cheeks to the fatty ends of the fins (so succulent that your lips will stick together with delight). The memory of it still haunts my dreams to this day.

1. Prepare your embers.

2. Scale and gut the fish, and remove the gills. Rinse briefly and dry well with paper towel.

3. Season the cavity of the fish and, in an enclosed grill rack, grill 15 cm (6 in) above evenly distributed embers for 8-10 minutes on each side until beautifully caramelised. The eyes should begin to pop.

4. Transfer the fish to a tray and allow to rest for 5 minutes.

5. In a small saucepan, bring the wine to the boil, and boil for 1 minute. Reserve.

6. Using scissors, cut the fish from tail to head along the lateral line (the seam that runs down the middle of the fish). With a spatula, push the flesh away from the spine to release the fillet and open the fish. Cut along the sides of the backbone and remove the spine and ribs. Season well with salt.

7. In a small saucepan, warm the olive oil and pour it over the fish. Add the lemon juice and white wine, and strain all the juices along with the oil back into the pan. Heat the liquid, whisking continuously to allow an emulsion to form.

8. Close the fish so it appears whole again, pour the emulsion over it, finish with the chervil and serve immediately.

RECIPE TYPE *savoury*

WOOD TYPE
apple

HEAT
medium-intense embers

ADDITIONAL EQUIPMENT
enclosed grill rack

INGREDIENTS

1 whole turbot, 2–3 kg
(4 lb 6 oz–6 lb 10 oz)

sea salt

50 ml (1¾ fl oz) dry white wine

200 ml (7 fl oz) fruity, mild extra-virgin olive oil, such as arbequina or koroneiki

juice of 1 lemon

½ bunch chervil, finely chopped

Eel

I have always been fascinated with eel, and not only from an eating perspective. While all ingredients have a story to tell, the story of eel is epic, with a 20-year life cycle that begins in the Sargasso Sea. What follows makes the eel the most mysterious fish in the world. Every year the larvae travel from their spawning grounds in the Sargasso Sea to Europe, a 6000 kilometre (3728 mile) journey along the Gulf Stream, which can take up to three years. They arrive in Europe in the winter – where they are known as 'glass eels' due to their transparent bodies – swimming upstream to begin their adult development. Ten years later, the eels return to the Sargasso Sea to spawn and die, thus starting the cycle again.

In the Basque country, glass eels are known as *angulas* and are worth their weight in gold, with each fish costing approximately one euro. While this doesn't seem much to pay for a whole fish, each juvenile specimen only weighs a gram, so a small bowl would typically set you back 100 euros ... needless to say it is the best seafood spaghetti you will eat in your life.

At Etxebarri, the start of the eel season was always awaited with eager anticipation. Traditionally they would be double cooked: blanched to remove the mucous membrane and then fried with chilli and garlic. While delicious, angulas often lose their unique texture and flavour in the process. Stored live they can survive in both fresh and salt water, but we found they survived best under a man-made waterfall with spring water channelled from the local mountain. We then killed them with a tobacco infusion (water infused with tobacco leaves), which saw them expel their mucous membrane, before washing them in spring water. They were then grilled directly in a basket over the embers. When it came to angulas, time stood still; they were so delicate and revered that everyone stopped whatever they were doing for the brief 45 seconds it took to cook them.

Such reverence for the eel is only matched by the Japanese. With their predilection for mastering just one skill, they have entire restaurants dedicated solely to preparing eel, and consume both saltwater (*anagi*) and freshwater (*unagi*) eel. The Japanese, however, import the baby eels and fatten them as if they're the wagyu of the sea until they are plump for the grill. They receive precise execution (ike-jime, page 246), as do all their fish. This is followed by unparalleled knife skills: the fish is split down the back, gutted and boned, butterflied and cut into square fillets. The eel then undergoes an extensive preparation involving skewering, steaming to remove excess fat, lacquering with a sweet soy sauce–based glaze and then grilling, more lacquering and more grilling. Known as *kabayaki*, the resulting fish is crisp on the outside and soft, fatty and tender on the inside.

The following preparation of eel pays a respectful nod to both cultures and is in accordance with how I like the majority of my seafood – killed, grilled and served immediately. While sansho pepper is a traditional Japanese seasoning for eel, the vibrant colour and tangy flavour of Australian native tamarind balances the fatty eel.

1. Prepare your embers and arrange a grill approximately 5 cm (2 in) above the embers.

2. Prepare the live eel. Place the eel in ice water for 20 minutes to slow down the heart rate. Carefully remove and, holding it firmly behind the head, place on a wooden board. Locate the point just behind the eye of the fish and firmly press a nail through the head, killing the fish immediately and securing the fish to the board. With a sharp knife, make an incision behind the head to sever the spine, which will allow the fish to bleed. Run the knife horizontally along the spine, opening the fish through the backbone. Butterfly open, removing the guts of the fish. Holding the knife flat, run it down the centre of the eel, keeping the blade parallel to the backbone. Remove the spine. Sever the head and tail and trim the fins. Cut the fish into quarters. Rinse quickly and dry well.

3. Prepare the tamarind. In a small saucepan, combine the tamarind and the sugar and cook over a gentle heat for 30 minutes until soft. Pass through a fine-mesh sieve into a clean container. Allow to cool to room temperature and reserve.

4. Thread the bamboo or metal skewers across the eel – this should keep it flat while cooking. Season the flesh of the eel with salt and sansho pepper. Grill, skin side down, over intense-medium embers for 3–5 minutes until caramelised. The fat should render from the skin, and the skin should become crisp.

5. Raise the grill to 20 cm (8 in) above medium-gentle embers, turn the eel and grill for a further 3 minutes. Season the skin side with salt. When cooked, the flesh of the eel will turn slightly opaque. Transfer to a clean tray and allow to rest in a warm place for 3 minutes.

6. Cut each fillet into 2 pieces and serve immediately with the native tamarind purée.

RECIPE TYPE *savoury*

WOOD TYPE
apple

HEAT
intense-medium to medium-gentle embers

ADDITIONAL EQUIPMENT
grill, wooden board the length of the eel, nail, 3 bamboo or metal skewers, 30 cm (12 in) in length

INGREDIENTS

1 live eel (freshwater or saltwater)

100 g (3½ oz) fresh or frozen Australian native tamarind, peeled (see Note)

70 g (2½ oz) sugar

sea salt

2 pinches of finely ground sansho pepper

NOTE

Gooseberries or tomatillos are a good alternative if Australian native tamarind is unavailable. Simply grill them until soft, then cook down with 20 g (¾ oz) of sugar.

003

Meat

200+ day
dry-aged beef rib

At odds with the typical grill restaurant, most of the menu at Firedoor comprises fish and vegetables. It is here that the largest variations continue to challenge me every day. Sometimes we have fourteen species of fish in the same week.

I knew, however, that if I was going to have one steak, it had to be a great one. It wasn't enough to simply take the best Australian steak and grill it. It had to be better. It had to contend with the memory of Galician beef, which is forever imprinted on my palate. The beef in Spain is recognised as some of the best in the world, with retired dairy cows producing rich, incredibly developed grass-fed beef.

Beef comes down to breed, feed and environment. Australia doesn't have the Spanish breed *rubia gallega*, nor the culture of using older animals that are exclusively and continually fed on rich pasture.

I wanted to produce a steak that would give me an emotional response, so I approached Anthony Puharich from Vic's Premium Quality Meat – a man as passionate about meat as I am about fire. We began exploring which breeds would work best.

Many of the old English breeds, such as angus and hereford, have been introduced into Australia. We hand-selected the best of these animals 12 hours after slaughter. What we found were ostensibly freaks of nature, pure breeds that had reached a level of intense marbling, a trait usually only found among wagyu. But it wasn't enough. We needed to take them to the next level. Taking inspiration from traditional Swedish preservation practices and Italian techniques for making prosciutto, we decided to render the fat surrounding the kidneys of the animal; we painted the open sides of beef with it until they were sealed under a layer of their own fat, before dry-ageing on the bone for more than 200 days (depending on the size, marbling and maturity).

As you can imagine, when we first began, it was an absolute nightmare. We had no information to go on and both the quality of the meat and the process were inconsistent. Over the next few years we persevered, we observed and we learnt, until we had something that was amazing.

Today we work with two main producers: Rangers Valley in northern New South Wales, which produce angus cattle that are grain-finished gradually for 270 days; and O'Connor Beef in Gippsland, Victoria, which breed grass-fed hereford-cross Angus cattle. Both produce very different expressions of the steak. In fact, no two animals are ever the same, and to this day I find it difficult to describe the flavour, with a profile ranging from intense umami meatiness through to old sherry and aged parmesan. We have created something so incredible and so unique that speaks of the ingredient and reminds me of what we achieved with the caviar all those years ago (see page 17). And the beautiful thing is that the process never ends. It is something that we continue to learn about and improve upon. It is an exceptional steak, but it takes a whole lot more than just me at the grill to bring it to the plate.

There are, of course, several ways to cook steak but there is so much going on with this steak that it needs very little embellishment other than the aromatic flavour of grapevines and good salt. It is important that the steak is brought to room temperature before cooking to allow the fats to render through the meat.
Continued on page 173 →

200+ day
dry-aged beef rib

SERVES 2-4

1. Prepare your embers. Suspend a grill approximately 10 cm (4 in) above the embers.

2. Holding the steak by the bone, brush it across the grill rack 3 or 4 times to baste the grill.

3. Place the steak on the grill and immediately season well.

4. Leave for 1 minute and rotate 60 degrees, adjusting the height of the grill or the embers as necessary to ensure that the steak is only being licked by flames.

5. Repeat the rotation 5 times until the surface is caramelised to a rich mahogany.

6. When ready, turn the steak and season again.

7. Repeat the rotation and adjustment process (steps 4-6).

8. Remove the steak from the grill and allow to rest in a warm place for 5 minutes.

9. With a sharp knife, remove the bone, trim the sinew line on the inside of the rib and carve into 5 mm (¼ in) slices. Serve immediately.

RECIPE TYPE *savoury*

WOOD TYPE
grapevines

HEAT
intense embers

ADDITIONAL EQUIPMENT
grill

INGREDIENTS
1 kg (2 lb 3 oz) dry-aged beef rib on the bone, at room temperature

fleur de sel or sea salt

Duck hearts
celeriac, sour cherry

SERVES 4

Duck hearts have to be one of the most undervalued and yet most tender parts of the bird. They are very approachable in terms of offal. With the Asian influences found in Australia, I wanted to create a play on peking duck, which is served in almost every restaurant in Chinatown. Instead of the entire duck, we go straight to the heart, grilling them on skewers with sour cherry sauce and spring onions. The whole lot is enveloped in grilled slices of charred celeriac to replace the traditional pancake (an idea inspired by acclaimed Danish chef Christian Puglisi, who uses the root to make a taco).

1. Prepare your embers.

2. Prepare the duck hearts. With a sharp knife, remove the top of the heart, clearing away any fat, sinew and arterial material. Place the duck hearts in the chilled brine solution and leave for 1 hour. Remove from the brine, rinse and dry carefully with a clean cloth.

3. Prepare the sour cherry sauce. Place the cherry stones between two pieces of paper towel and smash with a heavy-based pan or hammer. Reserve.

4. Combine the cherries, vinegar, coconut sugar, ginger, salt, cinnamon and lemon zest in a saucepan and bring to the boil. Simmer for 20 minutes until the fruit is completely soft. Remove from the heat and allow to cool slightly. Blend to a smooth purée, pass through a fine-mesh sieve into a clean pan, and bring to the boil. Add the broken cherry stones and cook over a low heat, stirring regularly, for an additional 1 hour or until thickened. Strain into a clean container and allow to cool.

5. Place the grill cooling rack directly on the embers. Grill the celeriac slices for approximately 2 minutes on each side until slightly charred and toasted. Brush lightly with some of the duck fat and keep warm.

6. On the same rack, grill the spring onions for 2 minutes until golden brown and lightly charred. Remove, season with salt and keep warm.

7. Meanwhile, thread the duck hearts on to the skewers (3 per stick) and grill for 2–3 minutes, brushing lightly with the remaining duck fat. Remove from the heat and season with salt.

8. Serve immediately with the charred celeriac pancakes, sour cherry sauce and grilled spring onions.

RECIPE TYPE *savoury*

WOOD TYPE
grapevines

HEAT
intense embers

ADDITIONAL EQUIPMENT
grill cooling rack, 8 metal skewers or bamboo skewers soaked in water for 2 hours

INGREDIENTS

24 duck hearts, peeled, trimmed and cleaned (see Note)

1 litre (34 fl oz/4 cups) Salt brine, 5% (page 240), chilled

1 celeriac, sliced 2 mm (1/12 in) thick (approximately 16 slices)

40 g (1½ oz) duck fat

12 spring onions (scallions)

fleur de sel or sea salt

For the sour cherry sauce

450 g (1 lb) cherries, pitted, reserving the stones

3 tablespoons aged red-wine vinegar

3 tablespoons coconut sugar

1 teaspoon freshly grated ginger

1 teaspoon salt

½ teaspoon ground cinnamon

1 teaspoon freshly grated lemon zest

NOTE
Like all offal, it is important to use fresh hearts sourced from a trusted supplier.

Beggar's chicken

SERVES 4

Chinese legend tells of a hungry beggar who stole a chicken in Hangzhou. Hotly pursued by the farmer, he made it as far as the river before concealing the bird in the mud. He returned at nightfall, lighting a small fire to cook his stolen dinner. When he retrieved the chicken he discovered it was encased in the rich clay of the riverbank, but he was so hungry he placed it directly on the embers. As the mud baked, a crust formed around the bird as it slowly steamed within. Breaking open the clay released an aroma so ethereal that it aroused the attention of the emperor, who was travelling on a nearby road. He stopped to eat with the beggar and deemed the rich succulence of the chicken to be delicious enough to grace the table of the Imperial Palace.

While this dish can seem elaborate – and you need to start it a day ahead – it is a beautiful way to cook directly in the fire and the results are worthwhile, with an unearthly tenderness that sees the meat fall away from the bone. It may be a kingly dish but, like a beggar, you will be compelled to eat it with your hands.

1. Prepare your embers.

2. Prepare the marinade. Lightly toast the spices in a cast-iron pan for 2–3 minutes until fragrant. Remove and grind the spices to a fine powder. Combine with the soy sauce, rice wine and ginger.

3. Wash the chicken and pat dry with paper towel. Rub the skin and cavity with the marinade. Cover and refrigerate for 6–8 hours.

4. Wash and soak the glutinous rice for 4 hours in filtered water. Rinse and then drain.

5. Remove the chicken from the refrigerator and drain, reserving the marinade.

6. Prepare the stuffing. Heat the grapeseed oil in a cast-iron pan and fry the garlic, ginger and spring onions for 1 minute until fragrant. Add the mushrooms and lap cheong, and continue to cook for 2 minutes. Add the day lilies, goji berries, dried scallops, drained rice and reserved marinade. Stir to combine. Remove from the heat and allow to cool.

7. Fill the chicken cavity with the stuffing, tying the legs together with kitchen string to secure. Place the chicken on one lotus leaf, breast side up. Fold the leaf over the sides and wings of the chicken onto the breast. Turn the wrapped chicken over, placing it on another lotus leaf and repeat the wrapping. Repeat once more with the third leaf, completely covering the chicken, before securing with butcher's twine.

8. Roll the clay into a rectangle about 5 mm (¼ in) thick. Place the wrapped chicken on one end of the clay, folding the other end over the chicken. Pinch the edges of the clay together with your fingers, ensuring that the chicken is well sealed. Leave to dry for 40 minutes.

9. Place the clay-wrapped chicken on a bed of embers, and completely cover the chicken with embers. Leave to cook in the ashes for 2 hours, at which point the clay will have baked hard on all sides. Remove the roasted chicken from the fire and allow to cool for 30 minutes.

10. Take to the table, break open the clay and unwrap the lotus leaves to reveal the magical bird.

RECIPE TYPE *savoury*

WOOD TYPE
ironbark

HEAT
gentle embers, hot ash

ADDITIONAL EQUIPMENT
cast-iron pan, butcher's twine, clay

INGREDIENTS

1 whole free-range chicken (1.8–2 kg/4 lb–4 lb 6 oz)

3 dried lotus leaves, soaked for 40 minutes until pliable

4 kg (8 lb 13 oz) earth clay

For the marinade

1 star anise

1 teaspoon cloves

1 teaspoon fennel seeds

½ cinnamon stick

1 teaspoon sichuan peppercorns

2 tablespoons soy sauce

60 ml (2 fl oz/¼ cup) shaoxing rice wine

2 teaspoons ginger root, finely minced

For the stuffing

50 g (1¾ oz/¼ cup) glutinous rice

1 tablespoon grapeseed oil

3 garlic cloves, finely minced

1 knob ginger root, finely minced

2 spring onions (scallions), finely chopped

50 g (1¾ oz) wood ear mushrooms, finely sliced

50 g (1¾ oz) shiitake mushrooms, finely chopped

2 lap cheong (Chinese dried sausage), diced

8 dried day lilies, soaked for 20 minutes in filtered water and finely chopped (optional)

1 tablespoon dried goji berries

10 g (¼ oz) dried scallops

Jurassic quail
toasted spelt, grapes

SERVES 4

Rest assured these birds do not come from the land that time forgot; they are the super-bird of the quail industry and the largest quail bred anywhere in the world. Australia does not possess a strong game culture, with limited availability creating only a small market. Environment and legislation mean that the majority of game is farmed and served relatively fresh, never to reach its fully ripened potential. Nor does Australia have the cornucopia of game birds found in Europe, where there are wild partridges, woodcocks, snipe, grouse and turtle-doves. These birds are so prized that the humble quail is often overlooked. By crossbreeding with native species of brown and stubble quail, Charlie and Carolyn Scott produced a unique bird that is large, succulent and, most importantly, full of flavour. The combination of quail and grapes harks back to Roman times. This recipe incorporates vines to produce embers, as well as leaves, which lend a slight citrus note against the rich quail.

1. Prepare the juniper syrup. Juice the grapes and then, in a small saucepan, bring to the boil and reduce the liquid to approximately 100 ml (3½ fl oz) until syrupy. Add the crushed juniper berries, remove from the heat and allow to stand for 6 hours or overnight.

2. Prepare the quail. For each quail, carefully peel back the skin covering the breasts and, with the point of a sharp knife, remove the wishbone. Gently fold the skin back. Using scissors, remove the wings, then cut down either side of backbone. Retain all bones for the stock, discarding any remaining offal. Clean and dry the bird thoroughly with paper towel. Turn the quail breast side up and push down firmly on the breastbone to flatten and splay the bird. Place the prepared quail in the chilled brine solution. Allow to brine for 2 hours. Drain, rinse and pat the quail dry with paper towel.

3. Prepare your embers.

4. Meanwhile, roast the quail bones (wings, wishbone and backbone) in a cast-iron pan over the embers until golden brown. Transfer to a large saucepan with the carrot, onion and chicken stock and bring to the boil. Simmer for 20 minutes, skimming off the scum from the surface. Remove and allow to cool slightly, then pass through a fine-mesh sieve into a clean pan.

5. Place the spelt in a medium saucepan, tossing to toast evenly until it starts to brown and become nutty. Season with sea salt. Remove and reserve.

6. In the same saucepan, add the olive oil and sweat the shallot and garlic until translucent and soft. Return the toasted spelt to the pan and stir to coat the grains in oil. Add two ladles of hot quail stock and bring to the boil. Simmer until almost all of the stock has evaporated. Add more stock, allowing it to evaporate; repeat for approximately 1 hour until the spelt is al dente.

7. Grill the quail, breast side down, in an enclosed grill rack approximately 15 cm (6 in) above the embers for 8-10 minutes until caramelised. Place two grapevine leaves on top of each bird and turn over. Cook the birds on top of the leaves for a further 5 minutes, brushing with juniper syrup. Transfer to a warm place to rest; the juices should run clear.

8. Grill the currant grapes in a fine-mesh sieve until they are about to burst.

9. Immediately serve the quail on top of the grapevine leaves with the spelt and grilled currant grapes.

RECIPE TYPE *savoury*

WOOD TYPE
grapevines

HEAT
medium embers

ADDITIONAL EQUIPMENT
enclosed grill rack, cast-iron pan

INGREDIENTS

4 Jurassic quail

2 litres (68 fl oz/8 cups) Salt brine, 5%, chilled (page 240)

1 carrot, cut into large dice

1 onion, cut into large dice

2 litres (68 fl oz/8 cups) chicken stock

8 grapevine leaves

200 g (7 oz) currant grapes on the vine

For the juniper syrup

500 g (1 lb 2 oz) green grapes

500 g (1 lb 2 oz) red grapes

2 tablespoons crushed juniper berries

For the toasted spelt

200 g (7 oz) spelt

sea salt

50 ml (1¾ fl oz) fruity, mild extra- virgin olive oil, such as arbequina or koroneiki

1 banana shallot, finely diced

1 garlic clove, minced

NOTE

The juniper berries need time to stand, so begin this recipe at least 6 hours ahead of time.

Bone marrow
sea urchin, purslane

SERVES 4

There is something a little primal and decadent about eating bone marrow with its creamy, almost custard-like richness that comes from the core of the animal. Bone marrow indicates the quality of the animal, so it is important to select bones from high-quality grass-fed cows.

Marrow has a nutty creaminess that can only be matched by the intensity of any accompanying ingredients, such as caviar or, in this case, sea urchin. This recipe combines earthy sweetness with the brininess of the sea for the ultimate surf and turf mouthful.

1. Place the shinbones in the chilled salt brine for 6 hours or overnight. Remove and pat dry with paper towel.

2. Ignite a fire in your wood-fired oven. Leave it to burn until medium embers are produced – you are aiming to bring the oven to a temperature of 300°C (570°F).

3. Prepare the sea urchins. Locate the surface with the central mouth and cut a large circular opening around it with a pair of sharp pointed scissors. Carefully remove the orange roe, which you will find hidden within. Rinse the roe in chilled filtered water and reserve. Discard the shell.

4. Prepare the dressing. Rinse the shallot in water and leave to soak in a bowl with the vinegar for 20 minutes. Drain the shallot well, add the lemon zest, capers, caper berries, fermented chilli paste, parsley and olive oil, and mix to combine.

5. Place the bone marrow in a cast-iron pan and roast in the wood-fired oven until the fat begins to render. The marrow is done when it turns a sienna-brown colour and starts to bubble around the edges.

6. Remove from the oven and brush the marrow with a spoonful of the fermented chilli and caper dressing. Top with the sea urchin and purslane. Serve immediately.

RECIPE TYPE *savoury*

WOOD TYPE
apricot or almond

HEAT
medium embers

ADDITIONAL EQUIPMENT
wood-fired oven, laser thermometer, cast-iron pan

INGREDIENTS

4 grass-fed shinbones, split lengthways (see Note)

1 litre (34 fl oz/4 cups) Salt brine, 5%, chilled (page 240)

3 live sea urchins (if unavailable, optional)

100 g (3½ oz) purslane, washed and picked

For the fermented chilli caper dressing

10 g (¼ oz) finely chopped shallot

50 ml (1¾ fl oz) chardonnay vinegar

zest of ½ lemon

20 g (¾ oz) capers, finely chopped

20 g (¾ oz) caper berries, finely chopped

½ teaspoon Fermented chilli paste (page 242)

¼ bunch flat-leaf (Italian) parsley, finely chopped

100 ml (3½ fl oz) fruity, mild extra-virgin olive oil, such as arbequina or koroneiki

---

NOTES

Ask your butcher to split your shinbones lengthways.

The shinbones need time to chill in the brine solution, so begin this recipe at least 6 hours ahead of time.

Lamb rump
borlotti, nettle

SERVES 4

Lamb rump cap, or chump, is an extremely underrated cut of meat, as it has a great balance of texture and flavour. Ask your butcher to leave the rump cap intact, with just the skin off, as it is the rich cap of fat that protects and bastes the meat as it cooks. When we began experimenting with dry-ageing lamb at the restaurant, we were really impressed at the difference that it made to the meat even after one week. The meat became softer with a richer, more pronounced lamb flavour. You may be able to find aged lamb but it is not strictly necessary.

Fresh borlotti beans have a nutty flavour and a creamy texture that is hard to replicate in this dish if using the dried beans. The vibrancy of the nettle finishes the borlotti with a fresh spinach-like flavour that is a tonic to the richness of the lamb rump.

1. Prepare your embers and arrange a grill directly over the top.

2. Prepare the lamb. Trim the excess fat from the rump cap, reserving the trimmings. With a sharp knife, score the fat cap on top of the rump, and leave to come to room temperature.

3. Place the borlotti beans in a cast-iron pan together with the carrot, celery, onion, fennel, leek, garlic and the reserved lamb trimmings.

4. Pour the chicken stock into the pan, bring to the boil, add a good glug of olive oil, season to taste and simmer gently for 40 minutes until the beans are tender. Remove from the heat and leave the ingredients to cool in the stock before discarding the vegetables and lamb trimmings.

5. In salted boiling water, blanch the nettles for 2–3 minutes until tender. Refresh in ice water and drain. Blend the nettles with a hand blender, adding a little water to form a smooth purée. Season, pass through a fine-mesh sieve and reserve.

6. Offset your embers, banking them up so they are parallel with the grill. Place the lamb rumps, fat side down, adjacent to and 10 cm (4 in) from the embers. Season well. Allow the fat to slowly render for 8 minutes or until the fat has caramelised.

7. Turn the rump caps and continue cooking for 5 minutes or until medium-rare. Season well and set aside in a warm place to rest for 8–10 minutes.

8. Warm the borlotti beans in stock, and add the nettle purée.

9. Grill the cavolo nero for 1 minute, season with sea salt and remove.

10. Slice the lamb rumps across the grain and serve immediately with the borlotti beans in nettle purée, cavolo nero and, if using, garlic flowers.

RECIPE TYPE *savoury*

WOOD TYPE
grapevines or olive

HEAT
offset, intense embers

ADDITIONAL EQUIPMENT
grill, cast-iron pan

INGREDIENTS

4 lamb rumps (caps on)

500 g (1 lb 2 oz) fresh borlotti (cranberry) beans, podded

1 carrot, halved

1 celery stalk, halved

1 large onion, peeled and halved

1 fennel, halved

1 leek, halved

2 garlic cloves

1 litre (34 fl oz/4 cups) chicken stock

extra-virgin olive oil (use a greener, peppery variety, such as leccino or picual)

sea salt

400 g (14 oz) nettles (see Note)

1 bunch cavolo nero, leaves picked and washed

12 garlic flowers (optional)

NOTE
Wear gloves while picking and washing nettle leaves, as they sting. If nettles are unavailable, you can use spinach instead.

Duck à la ficelle

À la ficelle (quite literally hanging 'by the string') is a traditional French method used for cooking legs of lamb, beef and poultry such as duck. The benefits are space-saving as the bird is suspended near the fire to cook slowly, leaving the embers free for cooking other dishes. It is also self-revolving, requiring only the occasional turn as it spins slowly by the fire. The dry heat of the fire gently renders the fat of the duck, leaving the skin to turn golden and crispy. For more about this technique, see page 40. In this recipe, the reduction of the kombu stock provides a salty umami kick to the sweet and sour glaze.

1. Prepare the duck, trimming the tips from the wings and removing any feathers and excess fat. Sliding your fingers under the skin, carefully separate the skin from the flesh. String your duck by the neck using butcher's twine.

2. Prepare the marinade. Lightly toast the fennel seeds and star anise in a medium saucepan and heat gently for 2–3 minutes until fragrant. Using a mortar and pestle, grind the spices to a fine powder.

3. Rub the duck cavity with the spices, orange zest and salt. Place the hay in the cavity and close the opening with a skewer.

4. Prepare the blanching liquid. Combine all the ingredients in a medium saucepan and boil for 5 minutes. Hold the duck by the neck above the pan and ladle the boiling liquid over the duck 5 times. This will open up the pores of the skin, allowing it to firm up and dry. Transfer the duck to a cooling rack and cool completely.

5. Prepare the glaze. Boil the blanching liquid until it has reduced to 50 ml (1¾ fl oz), then add the maltose and the vinegar. Boil, reducing to a thick glaze. Brush a layer of the glaze onto the duck's skin and allow to dry – the glaze will form a tacky layer. Repeat the glazing process to build up a bronzed layer. Leave to dry, uncovered, overnight on a rack in the refrigerator.

6. Prepare an offset fire (page 41).

7. Suspend the duck so that it is hanging by the neck 20 cm (8 in) in front of the fire and approximately 15 cm (6 in) above the ground, placing a pan below the duck to catch the fat as it renders.

8. Twist the string and release, allowing the duck to rotate evenly. Tend the fire as the duck cooks, moving the burning embers closer or further away as necessary.

9. Continue to spin the duck slowly for 2–3 hours, after which time the duck should be a rich mahogany colour and cooked through.

10. Once cooked, unhook the duck and rest for 10 minutes before serving.

RECIPE TYPE *savoury*

WOOD TYPE
cherry, handful of hay

HEAT
offset, intense embers

ADDITIONAL EQUIPMENT
butcher's twine, hook, 1 bamboo or metal skewer, grill cooling rack

---

INGREDIENTS

1 × 2 kg (4 lb 6 oz) duck, head on (see Notes)

For the marinade

1 teaspoon fennel seeds

1 star anise

zest of 1 orange

1 teaspoon sea salt

For the blanching liquid

1 litre (34 fl oz/4 cups) filtered water

110 g (4 oz) dried kombu

1 star anise

1 teaspoon fennel seed

peel and juice of 1 orange

For the glaze

100 g (3½ oz) maltose

100 ml (3½ fl oz) Pedro Ximénez vinegar or sherry vinegar

NOTES

The duck needs time to dry after being glazed, so begin this recipe a day ahead of time.

Ask your butcher for a duck with its head on, to make it easier to hang by the neck.

MEAT

Pork chop
sugarloaf cabbage, kombucha apple

SERVES 4

The timeless process of dry ageing can be used to improve the flavour and texture of many meats, including pork. At the restaurant we work with our butcher to dry age kurobuta pork loin on the bone for ten days with the skin on. The drying method intensifies the natural flavours, while the fat of the kurobuta pork (essentially a wagyu pig) mellows and melts like butter on the grill.

The combination of pork and apple is an English classic from my childhood. We would collect apples from our tree in the autumn (fall) and my mother would cook them down with just a little sugar to make a rich apple 'butter' for our pork. The acid from the naturally fermented kombucha gives this dish a tangy finish.

1. Prepare your embers and arrange a grill rack directly over the top.

2. In a large saucepan, combine the cold water, kombucha and sugar. Bring to the boil, stirring to dissolve the sugar.

3. Add the apples to the kombucha stock and simmer gently for 8-10 minutes until the apples are tender. Remove the pan from the heat and allow the apples to cool in the liquid.

4. With a sharp knife, score the fat of the pork chops at 1 cm (½ in) intervals.

5. Offset medium-intense embers, banking them up so they are parallel with the grill. Place the chops side by side on the grill, skin side down, adjacent to and 10-15 cm (4-6 in) from the embers (see page 41 for further details on indirect offset grilling). Season the rib side with salt.

6. Allow the fat to slowly render for 8 minutes until small bubbles form on the surface and the skin is golden and crisp. Rotate the pork chop to the bone side and cook for a further 8 minutes to conduct heat through the bone and ensure an even colour. Remove from the grill.

7. Rake your embers directly under the grill, and adjust the grill to sit 15 cm (6 in) above the embers. The embers should be bright orange. Place the pork face down on the grill, and season well. Adjust the height of the grill if necessary to ensure that the pork is only being licked by flames. Cook until the surface is caramelised to a rich mahogany colour. Turn the pork, season and repeat.

8. Remove and allow to rest in a warm place for 5 minutes.

9. Remove the apples from the liquid, remove the cores, and grill, cut side down, for 8 minutes until lightly caramelised.

10. Spray the cabbage quarters sparingly with olive oil and grill for approximately 4 minutes on each side until lightly charred. Remove, season and drizzle with the olive oil and apple wine vinegar.

11. With a sharp knife, remove the bone from the pork and carve the meat into 8 mm (¼ in) slices. Serve immediately with the grilled apples and cabbage.

RECIPE TYPE *savoury*

WOOD TYPE
cherry or chestnut

HEAT
offset, medium-intense embers

ADDITIONAL EQUIPMENT
grill

INGREDIENTS

1 litre (34 fl oz/4 cups) chilled filtered water

100 ml (3½ fl oz) kombucha

100 g (3½ oz) sugar

4 pink lady apples, halved

4 × 250 g (9 oz) pork loin on the bone, skin on

sea salt

1 sugarloaf or pointed cabbage, quartered

60 ml (2 fl oz/¼ cup) olive oil

30 ml (1 fl oz) apple wine vinegar

NOTE
Ideally you would want bone-in loins with the backbones removed and the ribs trimmed of meat (or 'frenched'). These are sometimes called pork racks.

Pork belly
roasted plum sauce

SERVES 4

Good pork belly is all about the crackling, and the satisfying sound it makes as it shatters like glass, giving way to the rich succulence that lies beneath. The fire provides the ideal dry heat for the perfect crackling, while the belly cooks slowly until smoky and tender. The alchemy of pairing meat with fruit goes back to medieval times and still resonates today, here with the tart ripeness of roasted plums served with pork.

1. Prepare your embers and place a grill cooling rack 15 cm (6 in) above the embers.

2. Prepare the plum sauce. Wash, halve and stone the plums. Grill, cut side down, over intense embers until caramelised. Transfer to a cast-iron pan, add the vinegar, chilli flakes, star anise, sichuan peppercorns, orange zest and juice, ginger and garlic. Bring to the boil then simmer gently, stirring occasionally until the plums are soft.

3. Pass through a large fine-mesh sieve. Return the mixture to the pan, add the soy sauce and the sugar and simmer, stirring until the sugar has dissolved. Continue to simmer for 5 minutes, taking care the mixture doesn't burn. It should be dark and glossy and taste sour, sweet, salty and fruity.

4. Place the pork belly on a grill cooling rack over a sink. In a medium saucepan, bring the water to the boil and carefully pour over it the pork belly to scald the skin – this will help to dry it out when cooking. Drain, pat dry and place in the refrigerator for 2 hours. Remove from the refrigerator and, with a sharp knife, score the skin evenly, with 1 cm (½ in) between each score, being careful not to cut into the flesh.

5. In a mortar and pestle, grind the star anise, sichuan peppercorns, orange zest, lemongrass stem and salt. Rub the mixture well into the underside of the pork belly (not the skin). Leave for 1 hour at room temperature.

6. Ignite a fire in your wood-fired oven. Leave to burn until the fire dies down, resulting in gentle embers. You are aiming to bring the oven to a temperature of 180°C (355°F).

7. Put the pork belly, skin side up, on a grill cooling rack to allow air to circulate around it. Sit the rack on a baking tray to capture fat and juices from the meat as it cooks. Slow roast the pork belly for 2 hours, rotating the pan after 1 hour to ensure even cooking.

8. Meanwhile, prepare the plums. Carefully remove the stones from the plums, coat the plums in the egg white, then roll in the caster sugar. Slow roast in a wood-fired oven at approximately 180°C (355°F) or in a cast-iron pan over the fire for 20 minutes until soft and caramelised with a crisp shell. Remove and allow to rest for 10 minutes, during which time the fruit will exude its rich ruby juices.

9. Remove the pork from the oven. Burn additional wood to raise the temperature of the oven to around 220°C (430°F), then roast the belly for a further 30 minutes until the skin is crisp and the meat is cooked through.

10. Remove from the oven and allow to rest for 10 minutes prior to carving.

11. Serve the pork belly with the roasted plums and roasted plum sauce.

RECIPE TYPE *savoury*

WOOD TYPE
cherry or chestnut

HEAT
intense embers, gentle embers

ADDITIONAL EQUIPMENT
grill cooling rack, cast-iron pan, wood-fired oven, laser thermometer

INGREDIENTS

1 kg (2 lb 3 oz) free-range pork belly, on the bone

500 ml (17 fl oz/2 cups) filtered water

2 star anise

½ teaspoon sichuan peppercorns

zest of 1 orange

1 lemongrass stem, smashed and chopped

10 g (¼ oz) sea salt

8 small blood plums or other variety of plums

1 egg white

30 g (1 oz) caster (superfine) sugar

For the plum sauce (see Note)

500 g (1 lb 2 oz) whole plums

200 ml (7 fl oz) red-wine vinegar

½ teaspoon dried chilli flakes

1 star anise

½ teaspoon sichuan peppercorns

zest and juice of ½ orange

25 g (1 oz) ginger, finely sliced

2 garlic cloves, sliced

25 ml (¾ fl oz) dark soy sauce

60 g (2 oz/⅓ cup) soft brown sugar

NOTE
The plum sauce will keep for up to 1 month in an airtight container in the refrigerator, so can be made in advance.

Goat

I love climbing mountains, the satisfaction coming not only from reaching the summit but, more importantly, from that sense of freedom in being among the hills and away from it all. While in France, I loved climbing in the alpine ranges, stumbling across alpine goats and sheep and the occasional herder living self-sufficiently in the hills and who, when asked, would invariably share some amazing cheese he had made. I continued climbing in Spain, and Victor and I would take to the mountains on the day the restaurant was closed. As well as being an escape from the grill, it brought us both back to nature with a greater understanding and appreciation of our local environment and the many ingredients that were growing around us.

My climbing took me to Argentina, where I had a strong desire to climb Aconcagua, the highest mountain in South America. At 6962 metres (22,841 feet) above sea level, it was quite an expedition with the walk into base camp taking several days. I was struck by the open pampas and the lifestyle of the gauchos who accompanied us. While we had our tents and expensive equipment, they gathered sticks and built a fire. The fire would bring them together; they gathered to cook various cuts of meat: lamb, goat or beef. I was drawn by the activity as much as the fire, so I sat with them drinking the peculiar brewed herb *mate* while they recounted stories from their lives.

The Argentinians favour a wood from the quebracho tree because it smokes very little. Quebracho is also one of the hardest woods in the world; its name is derived from the Spanish phrase '*quebrar hacha*', meaning 'axe breaker', giving an indication of how difficult it can be to harvest. However, the density means that it burns very slowly over a long period of time, making it ideal for cooking whole animals for several hours.

Of course *asado*, the name given to this style of cooking, is not limited to Argentina and can be found in several other countries and regions including Patagonia, Chile, Paraguay and Brazil, as well as Spain and Portugal.

Though lamb is mostly favoured, the spit roasting of goat goes back to the time of Virgil and may well be the earliest documented example of cooking an animal over fire. It is a timeless method, but one where the animal required continuous turning to ensure it is evenly cooked. The Argentine iron cross (*asado* cross), a large metal structure used to hold the carcase while it is cooking (see page 61) means you don't have to turn the goat continuously, as it is vertically splayed and positioned adjacent to the fire to cook slowly. The angle of the animal and its distance from the fire is adjusted in increments.

Cooking a whole animal over fire should be done slowly and cannot be rushed. The process renders the excess fat and results in succulent meat within and a caramelised crust on the exterior. The length of the process means patience is paramount – but the results are worthwhile.

Goat

SERVES 4

1. Build a firepit (see page 54).

2. Light a large fire and prepare your embers.

3. Prepare the goat. Crack the hip bone at each side to open at the leg end. Make an incision through the spine from the inside with a hacksaw and push firmly on either side so that the animal is splayed flat. Attach the goat securely to the cross or star pickets, threading the wire through the flesh of the legs close to the bone, to create tension when tied off with pliers to the iron cross. Thread wire through the spine and secure it to the cross to ensure the goat is supported during the cooking process. Suspend the animal, head down, at an angle of approximately 45 degrees to the ground, and 1.5–2 m (5–6.5 ft) away from the fire.

4. The fire should be offset in line with the hind legs of the animal. Using a rake, distribute intense embers around the base and sides of the cross, being careful to ensure that there is no fire directly below.

5. In a large saucepan, bring the water, wine, vinegar and salt to the boil, then add the crushed garlic. Remove from the heat and allow to cool. Use the tied bunch of rosemary as a brush: dip it liberally in the salt solution and slap the goat all over, releasing the aromatic oils of the rosemary.

6. Repeat the basting intermittently for the first 2 hours of cooking, giving the goat a beautiful salt crust as the fat renders.

7. Cook for 3–4 hours on the bone side, continuing to feed the fire, and rake the embers to ensure a continuous even heat.

8. After about 3 hours, you should see the shoulders start to bleed and the collagen start to give on the skin side, signalling that it is time to turn the goat over to the skin side.

9. Carefully turn the animal, placing it at an angle closer to the ground and cooking for a further 1 hour. The skin should turn a rich mahogany and have a beautiful thin crust that is hollow when tapped.

10. Using gloves, carefully remove the goat from the fire and rest it for 15–20 minutes on a large table.

11. Remove the goat from the cross. With a pair of tongs and a butcher's knife, divide the animal into forequarter, saddle and legs and then carve the succulent meat from the bone, working with one section at a time. Serve immediately.

RECIPE TYPE *savoury*

WOOD TYPE
ironbark or olive

HEAT
offset, intense embers

ADDITIONAL EQUIPMENT
hacksaw, asado cross or star pickets, thin wire, pliers

INGREDIENTS

1 milk-fed goat (cabrito or capretto), 8–10 kg (17 lb 10 oz–22 lb) (see Note)

1 litre (34 fl oz/4 cups) filtered water

1 litre (34 fl oz/4 cups) dry white wine

40 ml (1¼ fl oz) apple-cider vinegar

1 kg (2 lb 3 oz) sea salt

½ garlic bulb, crushed

1 large bunch rosemary, tied

NOTE

The goat should be young, milk fed and have an even coating of fat, which is necessary to withstand the long, slow cooking. Young milk-fed goat has a beautiful flavour, sweeter than young lamb, with pinkish, fine-grained flesh and a rich, even covering of milk fat. Boer goats are a South African variety that are now widely farmed worldwide and are prized for the quality of their suckling kids, aged at 40 to 60 days. Milk-fed rearing offers a tender, soft-textured and delicious red meat.

004

Fruit

Cherry tomato
stracciatella, black olive

SERVES 4

In this dish, the sweet flavour of cherry tomatoes is intensified by slow roasting to the point that they are almost candied, their thin leathery skins popping in your mouth. This is contrasted by the creamy quality of fresh stracciatella, a cheese you may recognise as the centre of burrata, and which spills forth when you slice into it. The meaty, intense empeltre olives have a wonderful crumbly texture when dried and give the stracciatella a salty tang.

1. Heat your wood-fired oven to 85–90°C (185–195°F).

2. Prise open the olives with your hands, removing the pits. Place on a baking tray lined with baking paper and allow the olives to slowly dry out in the oven for 2 hours, or until all the moisture has evaporated from the olives. Remove, allow to cool and coarsely chop into crumbs (see Note).

3. Cut the tomatoes from the vine and reserve the vine. Cut a shallow 'X' in the base of each tomato through the skin. Place the tomatoes on a tray and, using a blowtorch, scorch the tomatoes to remove the skins. Alternatively, the skin can be removed after blanching the tomatoes in boiling water for 5 seconds, then plunging them into iced water and draining.

4. Place the peeled tomatoes in a bowl, season lightly with sea salt and toss to coat.

5. In a small saucepan, combine the sugar and 50 ml (1¾ fl oz) of the tomato water. Heat gently until the sugar is dissolved, bring to the boil and cook until the liquid is very reduced and starts to turn a dark caramel colour.

6. Immediately remove the saucepan from the heat, add the remaining tomato water – the mixture will bubble up quickly – then stir to combine and place back over a low heat to reduce the liquid to a syrup.

7. Remove from the heat, add 1 reserved tomato stalk and 1 basil stem. Allow to cool and steep for 5 minutes.

8. Feed your wood-fired oven to increase the temperature to around 160°C (320°F).

9. Place the tomatoes on a grill cooling rack, calyx side down, and slowly cook in the oven for 1 hour, or until they shrivel and soften. Lightly spray with olive oil halfway through cooking.

10. Remove the tomatoes from the oven, immediately drizzle with the tomato caramel and leave to rest for 10 minutes.

11. Divide the stracciatella between 4 serving plates and season. Place 6 tomatoes on each plate, scatter with olive crumbs and garnish with basil leaves. Drizzle olive oil on the cheese to finish.

RECIPE TYPE *savoury*

WOOD TYPE
olive

HEAT
gentle embers

ADDITIONAL EQUIPMENT
wood-fired oven, laser thermometer, blowtorch, grill cooling rack

INGREDIENTS

100 g (3½ oz) empeltre olives, drained

24 cherry tomatoes on the vine

sea salt

100 g (3½ oz) caster (superfine) sugar

300 ml (10 fl oz) Tomato water (page 240)

2 basil stems, leaves picked and stems reserved

160 ml (5½ fl oz) extra-virgin olive oil, plus extra for spraying

300 g (10½ oz) stracciatella cheese, at room temperature

NOTE

The dried olives will keep for up to 6 weeks in an airtight container.

Tomato rice

SERVES 4

Paella is a traditional peasant dish from the town of Albufera in Valencia where rice has been grown on wetlands for 1200 years. It was introduced here by the Moors. Originally paella was cooked by the workers in the fields over an open fire, incorporating ingredients that were at hand. By burning grapevines or even orange wood, the rice would be infused with the smokiness from the fire. Citrus wood pairs well with the ripeness of tomatoes and the richness of the parmesan, but paella is first and foremost a rice dish so the quality of the rice itself is crucial. The best rice is said to come from Calasparra, a town in the neighbouring mountains of Murcia where it is grown along the Segura River. The cold clean mountain water slows the growth of the rice down, producing rice kernels that are drier with the ability to absorb three times the amount of liquid of other rice varieties.

Other than the rice, the most important elements of paella are the pan (from where the dish gets its name) and the stock, which in this case is the tomato water. The holy grail of any paella is the *socarrat*, the crisp golden layer that forms as the rice caramelises on the base of the pan. The flat, wide base of the paella is designed to cook the rice evenly while producing a good socarrat. Consequently it is important that the pan is sized in accordance with how many people you are cooking for.

The thin base of the pan does mean that the rice can burn easily if you're not careful. The ability to control the heat and cook a delicate rice dish over fire is one of the hardest skills to learn.

1. Prepare your embers and arrange a grill approximately 30 cm (12 in) above the embers.

2. Spread the embers evenly across the base of the grate.

3. In a paella pan, heat the olive oil and sauté the onion, garlic and chilli together with the fennel until soft. Add tomatoes, piquillo peppers, pimento, parmesan rind and a good pinch of salt, and stir in the rice ensuring the grains are well coated and form an even layer.

4. Carefully add the tomato water, stirring once to combine the ingredients. Simmer vigorously for 8-10 minutes, rotating the pan to ensure the rice cooks evenly.

5. Reduce the fire and allow the rice to cook gently for a further 15 minutes, being careful not to stir. The surface of the rice should be pitted with small holes.

6. Place the rosemary sprig and tomato leaves on top of the rice. Immediately cover with a clean, damp tea towel (dish towel), remove from the heat and leave to rest for 5 minutes.

7. Remove the tea towel and return the pan to the heat to create the soccarat, gently toasting the rice on the base of the pan for 5 minutes until it forms a golden crust.

8. Remove from the heat and serve immediately with torn parsley leaves, shaved parmesan and a generous drizzle of extra-virgin olive oil.

RECIPE TYPE *savoury*

WOOD TYPE
seasoned hardwood, preferably orange, burnt slowly down to embers

HEAT
medium-intense embers

ADDITIONAL EQUIPMENT
grill, paella pan

INGREDIENTS

100 ml (3½ fl oz) olive oil

1 onion, finely chopped

1 garlic clove, finely minced

1 red chilli, deseeded and finely chopped

1 fennel bulb, peeled and finely chopped

2 kg (4 lb 6 oz) vine-ripened tomatoes, peeled, seeds removed and diced (seeds and skins retained for tomato water)

2 piquillo peppers, finely chopped

1 teaspoon pimento (smoked paprika)

100 g (3½ oz) aged parmesan, shaved and rind reserved

sea salt

300 g (10½ oz) paella rice such as bomba calasparra rice

1 litre (34 fl oz/4 cups) Tomato water (see page 240)

1 rosemary sprig

4–5 pesticide-free tomato leaves from the vine

¼ bunch flat-leaf (Italian) parsley, leaves picked and torn

100 ml (3½ fl oz) light, fruity style extra-virgin olive oil such as arbequina or koroneiki

Mulberries

blueberries, smoked buttermilk ice cream

SERVES 4

We have a mulberry tree in our garden, and each spring it bursts into life with deep purple fruit. Mulberries only ripen on the tree, so they must be enjoyed in the moment and their short season is over all too quickly. I pick them with my wife and our son who sits on my shoulders, enabling him to reach the prized berries from the higher branches. Most berries are devoured straight from the tree, our fingers and lips stained a rich crimson, but some make it to the restaurant, where they are rolled with blueberries and gently kissed by fire over the dying embers, then accompanied by a rich and refreshing smoked buttermilk ice cream.

1. Prepare the ice cream base. In a saucepan, bring the cream to the boil with the vanilla pod. In a bowl, whisk together the egg yolks and sugar until pale, creamy and at ribbon stage (when the whisk is lifted from the bowl, the mixture will form thick ribbons). Continue whisking as you pour the boiling cream onto the egg and sugar mixture. Return to the pan and, stirring continuously with a wooden spoon, cook over a very gentle heat until the mixture thickens enough to coat the back of the spoon and reaches a temperature of 76°C (170°F).

2. Pass the mixture through a fine-mesh sieve into a clean bowl, allow to cool then chill.

3. Meanwhile, prepare your embers.

4. Once the ice cream base is completely chilled, stir in the buttermilk and transfer to an ice cream machine to churn until set.

5. Roll the blueberries in the sugar, allowing them just a light dusting, then remove.

6. Carefully place the mulberries and the blueberries in a fine-mesh sieve and grill over the embers for 1-2 minutes until the fruit is just on the point of bursting.

7. Remove the berries and serve immediately over the ice cream.

RECIPE TYPE *sweet*

WOOD TYPE
mulberry or other fruit wood

HEAT
gentle embers

ADDITIONAL EQUIPMENT
sugar thermometer, ice cream machine

INGREDIENTS

125 g (4½ oz) blueberries

20 g (¾ oz) caster (superfine) sugar

200 g (7 oz) mulberries

For the ice cream base

400 ml (13½ fl oz) Smoked cream (page 225)

1 vanilla pod, split

6 egg yolks

140 g (5 oz) caster (superfine) sugar

600 ml (20½ fl oz) buttermilk (page 227)

Pineapple
ginger and Thai basil sorbet

SERVES 4

Pineapples are the only edible member of the bromeliad genus known as *ananas*, which derives from a Tupi word meaning 'excellent fruit'. This is the reason pineapple is called *ananas* in most languages. English sailors likened the exterior of pineapple to a pine cone and the crisp juicy flesh to an apple. Because of its rarity, expense and visual attractiveness, the pineapple became the ultimate exotic fruit. They soon became a symbol of hospitality, and people would even hire some just to show off their social standing. Nowadays, pineapples are everywhere and are often grilled, as they develop a profound sweetness.

The ginger sorbet in this dish gives the pineapple a refreshing zing while the Thai basil adds a fragrant, savoury anise flavour.

1. Prepare your embers and arrange a grill approximately 20 cm (8 in) above the embers.

2. Prepare the sorbet. In a small saucepan, combine the water and glucose. Heat gently until the glucose is dissolved. Remove from the heat and allow to cool before combining with the ginger syrup, lime zest and juice and Thai basil. In a food processor or blender, blend for 1 minute before straining through a fine-mesh sieve. Chill. Transfer to an ice cream machine and churn for 30 minutes.

3. Prepare the pineapple. Retaining the top and leaves, peel the pineapple with a serrated knife. Remove the eyelets with a paring knife. Cut into quarters lengthways, slicing out the core from each quarter.

4. Place the pineapple quarters on the grill and cook for 2 minutes on each side until the pineapple becomes fragrant and dry. Continue grilling for a further 5 minutes on each side, brushing frequently with the ginger syrup until the sugars caramelise to dark amber. Transfer to a tray to rest.

5. In a small saucepan, boil the remaining syrup with the lime zest and juice until it is reduced and a dark caramel colour. Whisk in the smoked butter and brush over the pineapple.

6. Carve the pineapple and serve immediately with the ginger and Thai basil sorbet.

RECIPE TYPE *sweet*	
WOOD TYPE *stone fruit*	
HEAT *medium-intense embers*	
ADDITIONAL EQUIPMENT *grill, ice cream machine*	

INGREDIENTS

1 whole pineapple, top and leaves on

280 ml (9½ fl oz) Ginger syrup (page 243)

zest and juice of 1 lime

40 g (1½ oz) Smoked butter (page 227)

For the sorbet

400 ml (13½ fl oz) filtered water

60 g (2 oz) liquid glucose

150 ml (5 fl oz) Ginger syrup (page 243)

zest and juice of 2 limes

20 g (¾ oz) Thai basil leaves, picked and washed

Banana ice cream
smoked chocolate, honeycomb

SERVES 4

Banana, chocolate, honeycomb ... three simple ingredients that, when combined, produce the most satisfying dessert. Working on a low–refined sugar principle, the bananas are left to over-ripen, then they are grilled over a hot fire made of fruit wood. The bananas are then infused overnight in milk, which is strained and made into an ice cream. In this way, the entire fruit, including the peel, is used, intensifying the banana flavour. We use Valrhona Macaé, a dark chocolate containing 62 per cent cacao butter, to make a ganache. We make ours using water, instead of the usual cream, thanks to the work of French chemist Dr Hervé This. Cream tends to mask flavour and the result with ours is a lighter, cleaner taste and a ganache that melts luxuriously in the mouth. The water is also smoked over fruit wood, so it pairs beautifully with the dried fruit notes of the chocolate. The crisp texture of wildflower honeycomb completes the dessert.

1. Prepare your embers and arrange a grill approximately 15 cm (6 in) above them.

2. Prepare the ice cream. Grill the bananas, including the peel, over medium-intense embers for 5-10 minutes, turning halfway through until caramelised and blackened all over. Remove from the grill and blend with the milk. Place in the refrigerator and leave to infuse overnight.

3. Strain the banana milk and, in a small saucepan, combine with the glucose. Heat gently to 80°C (175°F). In a bowl, whisk the egg yolks and sugar until pale and creamy.

4. Set a clean container over ice. Whisking continuously, pour half of the warmed banana milk over the egg mixture. Once combined, pour the entire mixture back into the pan with the remaining milk and, stirring continuously, heat to 80°C (175°F). Remove from the pan immediately, straining the liquid through a fine-mesh sieve into the container set over ice. Cool to room temperature, then transfer to the refrigerator and chill.

5. Once chilled, churn in an ice cream machine. Transfer to a clean container and keep in the freezer.

6. Prepare the honeycomb. Line a small tray with baking paper. Place all the ingredients except the bicarbonate of soda in a medium pan and heat to 155°C (310°F) until it becomes an amber-coloured caramel. Immediately stir in the bicarbonate of soda, which will cause the mixture to bubble and foam. Carefully pour the hot mixture into the prepared tray. Allow to cool, then place in the freezer.

7. Prepare the chocolate ganache. Break the chocolate up in a bowl. In a medium saucepan, bring the smoked water up to a gentle boil and pour the water over the chocolate, allowing it to melt. Stir to combine, then whisk as it cools and emulsifies, continuing until it forms ribbons.

8. Divide the ganache between serving plates, break over shards of honeycomb and place a spoon or two of banana ice cream on each plate. Serve immediately.

RECIPE TYPE *sweet*

WOOD TYPE
stone fruit

HEAT
medium-intense embers

ADDITIONAL EQUIPMENT
grill, sugar thermometer, ice cream machine

INGREDIENTS

For the banana ice cream

350 g (12½ oz) over-ripe bananas

700 ml (23½ fl oz) full-cream (whole) milk

100 g (3½ oz) liquid glucose

6 egg yolks

100 g (3½ oz) sugar

For the honeycomb

140 g (5 oz) liquid glucose

60 g (2 oz) honey

400 g (14 oz) sugar

100 ml (3½ fl oz) filtered water

40 g (1½ oz) bicarbonate of soda (baking soda)

For the smoked chocolate ganache

175 g (6 oz) dark chocolate (at least 60% cacao solids, with notes of dried fruits, such as Valrhona Macaé 62%)

130 ml (4½ fl oz) Smoked water (page 241), preferably smoked with stone fruit wood

NOTE

The banana needs time to infuse the milk, so begin this recipe a day ahead of time.

Blood orange
upside-down cake

SERVES 6–8

Blood oranges have a rich crimson hue and a distinct, almost raspberry sweetness. Semolina flour provides texture, while a purée of blood oranges roasted in the fire imbues this cake with the warm flavour of caramelised citrus, which pairs wells with the exotic fragrance of cardamom. The rich caramel incorporates pomegranate molasses, which balances the sweetness and makes the sunset intensity of blood orange shine even brighter.

1. If using a Dutch oven, prepare your embers and set up a tripod over the fire. If using a springform cake tin, heat a wood-fired oven to 200°C (390°F).

2. Nestle 2 whole oranges in the ashes and bake for 20 minutes until charred on the outside and soft in the centre.

3. Remove the oranges from the ashes. Wipe the ash away and cut open to remove the seeds. Blend the oranges to form a purée. Reserve.

4. Grease a Dutch oven or springform cake tin and line with baking paper. If using a springform cake tin, cover the outside base and side with foil to stop the caramel from leaking out.

5. Prepare the caramel. Heat the pomegranate molasses, sugar, smoked butter and orange juice in a small saucepan over a medium heat, stirring until the sugar is dissolved and the mixture is smooth. Bring to the boil and cook, without stirring, for 4 minutes until the mixture has reduced and thickened. Pour the caramel into the base of the Dutch oven or cake tin and allow to cool completely.

6. Slice the remaining 2 oranges into 5 mm (¼ in) thick rounds. Arrange the orange slices in concentric circles in a single layer on top of the caramel, starting with larger slices around the edge and using smaller slices as you work towards the centre.

7. In a small frying pan, lightly toast the cardamom pods over a medium heat, remove the outer pod and crush the seeds in a mortar and pestle.

8. Prepare the cake. Beat the butter, sugar and crushed cardamom until light and fluffy. Add the eggs, one at a time, along with a tablespoon of semolina between each. Add the remaining semolina and the baking powder, and mix until combined. Add the orange juice, zest and burnt orange purée.

9. Pour the mixture into the Dutch oven, cover with the lid securely and suspend from the chain of the tripod over the burning embers. Alternatively, pour into the cake tin and place in the centre of the wood-fired oven. Bake for approximately 50 minutes. The cake is ready when a skewer inserted into the centre comes out clean. After removing from the heat, leave the cake in the Dutch oven or cake tin to cool for 10 minutes.

10. Run a knife around the edges of the cake, then turning over the Dutch oven or cake tin to remove the cake. Carefully place onto a wire rack to cool completely.

11. Serve with crème fraîche.

RECIPE TYPE *sweet*

WOOD TYPE
ironbark

HEAT
medium embers

ADDITIONAL EQUIPMENT
tripod and 23 cm (9 in) Dutch oven, or 23 cm (9 in) springform cake tin, wood-fired oven and laser thermometer

INGREDIENTS

4 blood oranges

6 cardamom pods

250 g (9 oz/1 cup) butter, diced, at room temperature, plus extra to grease

150 g (5½ oz) soft brown sugar

3 eggs

200 g (7 oz) fine semolina

1 teaspoon baking powder

zest and juice of 2 blood oranges

200 g (7 oz) crème fraîche, to serve

For the caramel

100 g (3½ oz) pomegranate molasses

100 g (3½ oz) soft brown sugar

50 g (1¾ oz) Smoked butter (page 227)

juice of 1 blood orange

NOTES

The blood orange purée can be made up to 3 days in advance and kept in the refrigerator. If blood oranges are not available, you can use navel oranges.

This can be made in a conventional oven; simply bake at 180°C (355°F).

Peaches
almond cream, barley crisp

SERVES 4

The summer months produce an abundance of stone fruit, with a rich cornucopia of peaches, nectarines, plums, apricots and cherries. They all partner well with almonds, partly because they belong to the same family. The natural flavour of peaches intensifies when grilled or roasted in a wood-fired oven, imbuing the flesh of the stone fruit with a sweet smokiness and accentuating its juicy ripeness. The almond cream provides a refreshing counterpoint with its floral fragrance of marzipan, created by the combination of the apricot kernel and the rosewater. Fresh green almonds have a jelly-like centre, while the barley provides a crisp cereal note.

1. Prepare your embers and arrange a grill approximately 20 cm (8 in) above the embers.

2. Prepare the almond cream. In a small saucepan, combine the water and sugar. Heat gently until the sugar is dissolved. Add the almonds and apricot kernels and blend until smooth. Stir in the rosewater. Soak the gelatine in cold filtered water for 5 minutes until soft before draining. Heat 100 ml (3½ fl oz) of the almond mixture, then stir in the gelatine until dissolved. Pour in the remaining almond mixture. Pass the mixture through a fine-mesh sieve into a clean container, allow to cool, then place in the refrigerator for 1½ hours until set.

3. Preheat the oven to 120°C (250°F). Line a baking tray with baking paper.

4. Prepare the barley crisp. In a medium saucepan, combine the barley with the water, bring to the boil and cook for approximately 30 minutes until soft. Drain the barley, retaining 100 ml (3½ fl oz) of the cooking liquid and, while still warm, blend with the butter to form a paste. Stir in the flour by hand, then refrigerate for at least 1 hour to allow the mixture to rest. Spread the mixture, using a spatula, onto the tray to a thickness of 1 mm (0.04 in). Bake in the oven for 15 minutes until golden brown and crisp. Remove and allow to cool.

5. Split the vanilla pod, scrape the seeds and place both the pod and the seeds in a small saucepan with the agave nectar. Heat gently for 10 minutes to infuse.

6. Brush the peach halves with the vanilla-infused agave nectar and grill, cut side down, for 6–8 minutes, allowing the sugars to gradually caramelise. Transfer to a tray to rest, brushing with more of the syrup.

7. Peel and halve the green almonds.

8. Serve the peaches warm with the roasting juices and spoonfuls of the almond cream between the peaches. Break the crisp into rough shards and place between and around the peaches. To finish, scatter with the green almonds and, if using, elderflowers.

RECIPE TYPE *sweet*

WOOD TYPE
almond

HEAT
medium-intense embers

ADDITIONAL EQUIPMENT
grill or wood-fired oven, laser thermometer

INGREDIENTS

¼ vanilla pod

100 ml (3½ fl oz) agave nectar

4 ripe peaches, halved and stones removed

200 g (7 oz) green almonds

elderflowers (optional)

For the almond cream

800 ml (27 fl oz) filtered water

60 g (2 oz) caster (superfine) sugar

270 g (9½ oz/1¾ cups) blanched almonds

30 g (1 oz) blanched apricot kernels

1 teaspoon rosewater

2 leaves titanium gelatine

For the barley crisp

40 g (1½ oz) barley flakes

500 ml (17 fl oz/2 cups) filtered water

35 g (1¼ oz) unsalted butter

20 g (¾ oz) plain (all-purpose) flour

ALTERNATIVE METHOD
Roast the peaches in a wood-fired oven heated to 120°C (250°F).

FRUIT

Cape gooseberry pavlova
elderflower cream

SERVES 6–8

There is something truly magical about the simplicity and delight of pavlova. It was a treat when I was growing up, and is the one dish that I've never been able to make as well as my mother, despite all my wild attempts. As a child, I was as fascinated by the process as much as the beauty of the finished pudding. My mother would always make pavlova just before going to bed, whipping the egg whites and sugar to dreamy cloud-like peaks before slow-baking in the oven. Dressed in her robe, she would sit up and wait with a cup of tea and a crossword, turning the oven off after an hour, strictly forbidding the oven door to be opened until the morning. Once served, the dry and crisp exterior would shatter, giving way to the mallowy middle.

The intense heat and dryness of a wood-fired oven provides the ideal conditions for the perfect meringue. Cape gooseberries have a vibrant sweet sourness and a ripe earthiness that pairs well with this sugary meringue.

1. Start a fire in your wood-fired oven and bring the heat to 120°C (250°F). Line a baking tray with baking paper.

2. Prepare the pavlova. Whisk the egg whites with 50 g (1¾ oz) of the caster sugar until soft peaks form. Continue whisking, gradually adding the remaining sugar in stages until the sugar has dissolved and the meringue is glossy, thick and stiff. Add the vinegar and gently fold through the cornflour.

3. Spoon the mixture onto the tray and place in the back of the wood-fired oven. Bake for approximately 1½ hours.

4. Move the pavlova from the back of the oven to the front and leave the door open a crack to allow a small amount of air to escape. Leave the pavlova to sit for at least 6 hours, or overnight if possible, to allow it to set and dry sufficiently.

5. Prepare the custard base for the fool. Heat the milk in a small saucepan. In a bowl, whisk the egg yolks with the sugar until creamy. Pour the egg yolks over the hot milk, whisking continuously, then strain into a clean saucepan and cook over a gentle heat until the mixture is thickened and coats the back of a spoon. Remove from the heat and allow to cool.

6. Grill 200 g (7 oz) of the cape gooseberries in a fine-mesh sieve until slightly smoky and bursting. Transfer to a bowl and break up lightly using a fork to create a rough paste.

7. Whip the double cream to soft peaks with the elderflower cordial. Carefully fold in the gooseberry paste and the custard, creating a rippled effect. Transfer to a container and chill.

8. Before serving, grill the remaining cape gooseberries in the same way as above.

9. Serve the pavlova with the gooseberry elderflower fool, top with grilled cape gooseberries and, if using, elderflowers.

RECIPE TYPE *sweet*

WOOD TYPE
stone fruit

HEAT
gentle embers

ADDITIONAL EQUIPMENT
wood-fired oven, laser thermometer

INGREDIENTS

For the pavlova

250 g (9 oz) egg whites

375 g (13 oz/1⅔ cup) caster (superfine) sugar

1 teaspoon white vinegar

1 teaspoon cornflour (cornstarch)

For the cape gooseberry fool

150 ml (5 fl oz) full-cream (whole) milk

2 egg yolks

30 g (1 oz) sugar

300 g (10½ oz) cape gooseberries

150 ml (5 fl oz) thick (double) cream

50 ml (1¾ fl oz) Elderflower cordial (page 243)

fresh elderflowers (optional)

Coconut
chocolate, cherry granita

SERVES 4

While botanically a coconut is a drupe and not a true nut, coconuts have a rich nutty flavour and creamy texture that is a good substitute for the richness of dairy. Like the process of slowly cooking a tin of condensed milk and making dulce de leche, the idea was that, buried in the ashes, the coconut flesh would cook down slowly in its own sweet milk. The result was incredible. The coconut retained all its natural juices but they had combined with the creamy flesh, taking on subtle notes of smoke and caramel, and an intense coconut flavour. We then froze it to make a refreshing sorbet, which needed nothing more than the addition of a little sugar. For a bit of texture, we made a choc-top, combining high-quality chocolate with coconut oil, which sets and hardens to a crisp coating on contact and provides a delicate bitterness to the sweetness of the coconut. A chocolate with notes of dried fruit pairs well with the fresh cherry granita and grilled cherries, making it quite decadent.

1. Prepare your embers.

2. Toast the coconuts directly on medium-intense embers until blackened all over, covering the coconuts in 200°C (390°F) hot ashes. Leave to cook for 2 hours, then remove and allow to cool.

3. Carefully make a hole in the top of each coconut and strain the coconut water into a container. This should yield 400 ml (13½ fl oz) of liquid.

4. With a hacksaw, cut the tops off the coconuts. Scoop out the flesh; you should have approximately 600 g (1 lb 5 oz). Place the coconut shells in the freezer.

5. Blend the reserved coconut water with the flesh to form a smooth purée. Pass through a fine-mesh sieve into a bowl, add the glucose and combine. Refrigerate the mixture for 8 hours. Once the mixture has cooled completely, churn it in an ice cream machine. Transfer to a container and keep in the freezer.

6. Prepare the granita. Boil the sugar and water until the sugar is dissolved, producing a light syrup. Allow to cool completely. Blend the cherries to a smooth purée, adding the sugar syrup, salt and a squeeze of lemon. Place in a clean shallow container and freeze for at least 1 hour.

7. Prepare the chocolate-top liquid. Melt the chocolate in a bowl suspended over a pan of barely simmering water. Remove from the heat and whisk in the coconut oil until emulsified.

8. With a fork, scrape shavings from the cherry granita. Return to the freezer.

9. Remove the charred coconut shells from the freezer and place a large scoop of coconut sorbet in the middle of each shell. Carefully spoon over the chocolate-top liquid (whisking first to re-emulsify if it has separated). Place in the freezer for 2 minutes to harden.

10. In a fine-mesh sieve, grill the halved cherries over gentle embers until warm, slightly smoky and the juices are just beginning to release.

11. Remove the granita from the freezer, scrape again with a fork, and then place the granita around the dome of each coconut choc-top. Surround with warm grilled cherries and serve immediately.

RECIPE TYPE *sweet*

WOOD TYPE
cherry

HEAT
medium-intense embers, hot ash, gentle embers

ADDITIONAL EQUIPMENT
hacksaw, ice cream machine

INGREDIENTS

2 coconuts (approximately 1.2 kg/ 2 lb 10 oz each) (see Notes)

150 g (5½ oz) liquid glucose

100 g (3½ oz) dark chocolate (at least 60% cocoa solids, such as Valrhona Macaé 62%)

50 g (1¾ oz) coconut oil

100 g (3½ oz) ripe, sweet cherries, washed, pitted and halved

For the granita

75 g (2¾ oz) caster (superfine) sugar

150 ml (5 fl oz) filtered water

250 g (9 oz) ripe, sweet cherries, washed and pitted

pinch of sea salt

squeeze of lemon juice

NOTES

The coconut mixture needs time to chill before churning, so begin this recipe at least 8 hours ahead of time.

Be sure to use fresh coconuts that are heavy for their size.

FRUIT

Rhubarb vanilla marshmallows

One of the best things about cooking over the fire is gathering with friends and family to share in the experience, telling stories and passing on knowledge. With that in mind, here is a recipe for marshmallows that was kindly shared with me by Rob Kabboord, Chef de Cuisine at Quay in Sydney. I love how the tangy flavour of rhubarb cuts through the sweetness of the meringue. And what better dessert to share around the campfire than toasted marshmallows.

1. Split the vanilla pod, scrape the seeds and place the pod and the seeds in a small saucepan with the rhubarb and 100 g (3½ oz) of the caster sugar. Cover with a lid and cook over a low heat, stirring occasionally until the rhubarb is really soft. Blend to a smooth purée and pass through a fine-mesh sieve.

2. Soak the gelatine in a bowl of cold filtered water for 5 minutes until soft.

3. Pour half of the rhubarb purée into a clean saucepan and bring to the boil. Remove the pan from the heat, drain the softened gelatine leaves and add to the pan. Stir until dissolved, then stir in the remaining rhubarb purée.

4. Place the filtered water and the remaining caster sugar in a saucepan and heat to 120°C (250°F).

5. Remove the pan from the heat, wait 1 minute and then add the rhubarb purée.

6. Whisk the egg whites with a pinch of salt until firm peaks form.

7. Add the rhubarb syrup mixture to the egg whites a little at a time, whisking continuously until all of the fruit is incorporated and the mixture is thick enough to hold its shape.

8. Mix together the icing sugar and the cornflour. Use this mixture to dust a baking tray lined with baking paper.

9. Spread the marshmallow mixture to a thickness of 3 cm (1¼ in) onto the baking tray and then sprinkle the icing sugar and cornflour mixture over the top (reserving a little). Place in the refrigerator to firm for at least 8 hours or overnight.

10. Combine the ingredients for the sherbet mixture. Dust a cook's knife with the remaining icing sugar/cornstarch mixture and cut the marshmallows into cubes. Roll the cubes in the sherbet mixture, and toast over a fire.

RECIPE TYPE *sweet*

WOOD TYPE
any

HEAT
gentle embers

ADDITIONAL EQUIPMENT
sugar thermometer

INGREDIENTS

½ vanilla pod

200 g (7 oz) rhubarb stalks, roughly chopped

500 g (1 lb 2 oz) caster (superfine) sugar

7 sheets gold gelatine

125 ml (4 fl oz/½ cup) filtered water

4 large egg whites

pinch of salt

3 tablespoons icing (confectioners') sugar

2 tablespoons cornflour (cornstarch)

For the sherbet mixture

100 g (3½ oz) icing (confectioners') sugar

1 teaspoon citric acid

1 teaspoon baking powder

NOTE

The marshmallow mixture needs time to firm, so begin this recipe at least 8 hours ahead of time.

Quinces
mascarpone, pistachio

SERVES 4

The smell of ripe quince is intoxicating: a heady, perfumed scent of vanilla, citrus and apple, which speaks of the autumnal treasure that lies deep within. Its astringency means that it is not pleasant to eat raw but, cooked slowly, it not only magically transforms from yellow to a deep ruby red but its flavour takes on a wonderful sweet intensity. Here, the honeyed notes of mead provide a natural sweetness and richness that is perfectly balanced by the fresh mascarpone.

1. Peel, halve and core the quinces, reserving the peelings and cores.

2. Wrap the trimmings in muslin (cheesecloth) and place in a large saucepan. Split the vanilla pod, scrape the seeds and place the pod and the seeds in the saucepan with the mead, water, honey, cinnamon and orange zest.

3. Submerge the quinces in the liquid and, over a low heat, simmer for approximately 6 hours until they become a rich burgundy colour and are very tender.

4. Prepare your embers and arrange a grill 15 cm (6 in) above the embers.

5. Add a couple of rosemary sprigs (retaining the woody stems for grilling) to the quince saucepan. Remove from the heat and allow the quinces to cool in the poaching liquid.

6. Strain the liquid into a saucepan and boil it to reduce to a syrup consistency.

7. Meanwhile, grill the quinces, cut side down, adding the remaining rosemary stems to the embers for additional fuel and flavour. Brush the reduced syrup on the quinces during the cooking process.

8. Serve with fresh mascarpone, grated fresh pistachio and picked rosemary flowers.

RECIPE TYPE *sweet*

WOOD TYPE
apple

HEAT
medium embers

ADDITIONAL EQUIPMENT
muslin (cheesecloth), grill

INGREDIENTS

4 quinces

½ vanilla pod

750 ml (25½ fl oz/3 cups) mead

250 ml (8½ fl oz/1 cup) filtered water

20 g (¾ oz) honey

1 cinnamon stick

zest of 1 orange

½ bunch flowering rosemary, flowers picked

mascarpone or Smoked mascarpone (page 225)

fresh pistachios

NOTE
The quinces need time to simmer, so begin this recipe at least 6 hours ahead of time.

Pear and lemon thyme bellini

SERVES 1

Bellinis are the aperitif of choice for entertaining as they always please a crowd, being fresh and fruity. This drink is great all-year round as the brandy warms the soul in winter and the fresh lift of prosecco makes it a perfect summer tipple.

1. Prepare your embers and place a grill cooling rack 15 cm (6 in) above the embers.

2. Prepare the pear purée. Grill the pear, cut side down, until coloured. Place in a saucepan with the water and brown sugar and bring to the boil. Poach for 20 minutes until the pears have softened. Remove the pears and, with a hand blender, purée with the syrup until smooth and creamy. Pass through a fine-mesh sieve and chill until needed.

3. Prepare the cocktail. Add the brandy, lemon and pear purée to a cocktail shaker and shake.

4. Strain into a champagne flute, top with prosecco and the lemon thyme sprig to garnish.

RECIPE TYPE *drink*

WOOD TYPE
apple or pear

HEAT
medium embers

ADDITIONAL EQUIPMENT
grill cooling rack, cocktail shaker

INGREDIENTS
For the cocktail

30 ml (1 fl oz) brandy

15 ml (½ fl oz) fresh lemon juice

2 tablespoons corella pear purée

100 ml (3½ fl oz) prosecco

1 lemon thyme sprig, to garnish

**For the corella pear purée
(makes 120 g/4½ oz)**

1 corella pear (or other variety), cored and halved lengthways

50 ml (1¾ fl oz) filtered water

50 g (1¾ oz) soft brown sugar

Lemon pisco sour

SERVES 1

A good pisco sour is one of my all-time favourite drinks. Grilling the lemon gives you more of a pisco sweet and sour, as the tangy lemons caramelise and mellow. This recipe uses an oak-aged Chilean pisco, which has a naturally sweeter finish than Peruvian pisco, so less sugar is needed.

1. Prepare your embers and place a grill cooling rack 10 cm (4 in) above the embers.

2. Grill the lemon halves, cut sides down, until gently caramelised.

3. In a cocktail shaker, add the pisco, sugar syrup, egg white and plenty of ice.

4. Squeeze the grilled lemon over the ice in the cocktail shaker and shake vigorously.

5. Strain into a chilled glass, finish with bitters and serve.

RECIPE TYPE *drink*

WOOD TYPE
fruit wood

HEAT
medium embers

ADDITIONAL EQUIPMENT
grill cooling rack, cocktail shaker

INGREDIENTS

1 lemon, halved

60 ml (2 fl oz/¼ cup) pisco, such as Capel oak-aged double-distilled

15 ml (½ fl oz) sugar syrup

1 egg white

ice cubes

3 drops aromatic bitters

Grilled ginger daiquiri

SERVES 1

The daiquiri is a much maligned drink, often resembling a kids' slushie. Its real beauty lies in the careful balance of three simple ingredients; rum, lime juice and sugar. The addition of grilled ginger introduces a fragrant heat to the drink.

1. In a cocktail shaker, add the rum, lime and ginger syrup with ice and shake hard.

2. Strain into a frozen cocktail glass and garnish with a wheel of lime on the rim.

RECIPE TYPE *drink*	

ADDITIONAL EQUIPMENT
cocktail shaker

INGREDIENTS

60 ml (2 fl oz) aged rum

30 ml (1 fl oz) lime juice

15 ml (½ fl oz) Ginger syrup (page 243)

ice cubes

lime slice, to garnish

Poblano caipirinha

SERVES 1

Poblano caipirinha is a reinterpretation of a caipirinha blending the distinct flavour of cachaça with smoky and grassy grilled poblano chillies. Sweet spice from the cumin rounds out this unique and refreshing cocktail.

1. Prepare your embers and place a grill cooling rack 15 cm (6 in) above the embers.

2. Grill the lime halves, cut sides down, with the poblano chillies until caramelised and lightly charred.

3. Cut the poblanos into 3 pieces and steep in the cachaça for 2 hours.

4. Prepare the cumin syrup. In a small saucepan, bring the sugar, water and cumin seeds to the boil over a medium heat. Simmer for 10 minutes, remove and allow to cool completely.

5. In a cocktail shaker, add the cachaça, grilled lime juice, cumin syrup and ice, and shake hard.

6. Strain into a frozen cocktail glass and garnish with the poblano.

RECIPE TYPE *drink*

WOOD TYPE
ironbark

HEAT
medium-intense embers

ADDITIONAL EQUIPMENT
grill cooling rack, cocktail shaker

INGREDIENTS

For the cocktail

60 ml (2 fl oz/¼ cup) poblano cachaça

30 ml (1 fl oz) grilled lime juice

10 ml (¼ fl oz) cumin syrup

ice cubes

thin sliver poblano chilli, to garnish

For the grilled lime juice

1 lime, halved

For the poblano cachaça (makes 700 ml/23½ fl oz)

3 poblano chillies

700 ml (23½ fl oz) cachaça

For the cumin syrup (makes 300 ml/10 fl oz)

200 g (7 oz) soft brown sugar

200 ml (7 fl oz) filtered water

1 teaspoon cumin seeds

Grilled peach iced tea

SERVES 4

There's nothing more refreshing than a cup of tea, and this is a great cooler to whip up on a hot day. The floral notes in French Earl Grey, which include hibiscus flowers, sunflowers and rose petals, pair well with grilled stone fruit such as peaches, particularly as peach is a member of the rose family.

1. Prepare your embers and arrange a grill cooling rack approximately 15 cm (6 in) above the embers.

2. In a medium saucepan, bring the water to a boil, then remove from the heat. Add the tea leaves and steep for 2 minutes. Strain the tea into a large jug.

3. Add the agave nectar and the lemon thyme sprigs, stirring to combine.

4. Add half the ice and allow to cool.

5. Grill the peach halves, cut side down, until caramelised and slightly charred. Remove from the grill and slice each half into 4 pieces. Add the peach slices to the tea.

6. Stir in the lemon juice and the remaining ice. Serve immediately.

RECIPE TYPE *drink*	
WOOD TYPE *peach*	
HEAT *medium-intense embers*	
ADDITIONAL EQUIPMENT *grill cooling rack*	

INGREDIENTS

1 litre (34 fl oz/4 cups) filtered water

5 g (¼ oz) French Earl Grey tea leaves

600 ml (20½ fl oz) agave nectar

3 lemon thyme sprigs

1 kg (2 lb 3 oz) ice cubes

2 yellow peaches, halved and stones removed

120 ml (4 fl oz) fresh lemon juice

Chestnut roasted negroni

SERVES 1

The negroni is a cocktail with an ever-increasing following, as its bittersweet and botanical scent enchant the sophisticated tippler. Here, the all-Italian drink is imbued with the flavours of the autumnal chestnut. The oil transferred from the chestnuts into the sweet vermouth gives the drink an unctuous finish. Look for firm, smooth, glossy chestnuts that are free from blemishes. The chestnut syrup will keep refrigerated for up to six weeks.

1. Prepare your embers.

2. Using a paring knife, score the chestnuts through the tough exterior, running the knife around the entire equator. This will ease the peeling process and allow steam to escape during cooking, preventing them from exploding. Place the chestnuts in a fine-mesh sieve and roast them for 30 minutes, agitating the pan every now and then. Remove and allow to cool enough to handle.

3. Peel the nuts and place in a saucepan with the water. Bring to the boil and simmer for 10 minutes. Add the sugar and cook over a medium heat for 5 minutes, until reduced to a syrup. Remove from the heat, allow to cool and refrigerate until required.

4. Prepare the negroni. In a frozen glass, stir the gin, campari, vermouth and chestnut syrup over ice for 30 seconds until diluted. Garnish with the orange peel and serve.

RECIPE TYPE *drink*	
WOOD TYPE *chestnut*	
HEAT *intense embers*	

INGREDIENTS

30 ml (1 fl oz) gin

30 ml (1 fl oz) campari

30 ml (1 fl oz) sweet vermouth

ice cubes

long strip of orange peel, to garnish

For the chestnut syrup (makes 500 ml/17 fl oz/2 cups)

100 g (3½ oz) chestnuts

500 ml (17 fl oz/2 cups) filtered water

200 g (7 oz) caster (superfine) sugar

005

Dairy

Ember-baked cheese

It is hard to think of cheeses as seasonal goods, but quality cheese is all about the richness of the pasture. Vacherin Mont d'Or, for example, is only made in the winter months when the cows come down from *alpage* (mountain pastures) and are fed hay instead of fresh grass. The resulting cheese is an undulating orange rind encasing a sweet, runny and truly magical cheese. As this cheese ripens in its cedar box, it develops a unique nutty aroma and a richness that makes it perfect for baking in the dying embers of a wood fire.

1. Prepare your embers, which are best if they are slowly smouldering.

2. Remove all plastic packaging, keeping the cheese inside its cedar box.

3. With the point of small knife, make 5 incisions, evenly dispersed, in the top of the cheese and in each one insert a rosemary sprig.

4. Arrange a small bed of embers directly under and around the cheese and bake for 10-12 minutes until the cheese is warm and runny inside. Best eaten with a spoon.

RECIPE TYPE *savoury*
WOOD TYPE *stone fruit*
HEAT *gentle embers*
INGREDIENTS 1 Vacherin Mont d'Or or a similar creamy, rinded cheese in a cedar box   5 rosemary sprigs

Smoked ricotta

MAKES 500 G (1 LB 2 OZ)

The beauty of ricotta lies in its creamy versatility. It can be used in both sweet and savoury applications, has a variable texture (either soft or firm) and can be served fresh or cooked. Originally a by-product from cheesemaking (ricotta means 'recooked'), ricotta is an Italian whey cheese that dates back to the Bronze Age.

There are several types of ricotta, including, most interestingly, a smoked (*affumicata*) ricotta that is made by smoking it over oak, beech or chestnut wood until it develops a grey crust.

To make a soft creamy cheese, this recipe smokes the milk first, which also ensures a delicate harmony between the flavour of the wood and the flavour of the milk.

1. In a large saucepan, combine the smoked jersey milk and smoked cream. Heat to 90°C (195°F), gently stirring to prevent scorching.

2. Remove from the heat and add the fresh lemon juice. Immediately stir once to combine the lemon juice and then stop. Stirring too much will result in smaller and very granular curds in the ricotta.

3. Leave to sit for 10-15 minutes to allow the curds to separate from the whey.

4. Carefully transfer the curds and whey to a fine-mesh sieve lined with muslin (cheesecloth) placed over a bowl.

5. Leave to drain for at least 2 hours. Check the texture of the ricotta, which should be creamy. Retain the whey for other uses, such as in baking, dressings, brines and pickles.

6. Before serving, season with salt as desired, finishing with fresh lemon zest and juice.

RECIPE TYPE *base*

WOOD TYPE
chestnut

HEAT
indirect, gentle embers

ADDITIONAL EQUIPMENT
sugar thermometer, muslin (cheesecloth)

INGREDIENTS

750 ml (25½ fl oz/3 cups) jersey milk

125 ml (4 fl oz/½ cup) Smoked cream (opposite)

2 tablespoons fresh lemon juice

sea salt

zest and juice of ½ lemon

NOTES

Although best enjoyed the day it is made, fresh ricotta will keep for up to 4 days in the refrigerator.

The whey will also keep for up to 4 days in the refrigerator or for up to 6 months in the freezer.

Smoked mascarpone

MAKES 300 G (10½ OZ)

The buttery richness of fresh mascarpone is balanced by its fresh acidity, making it suitable for a variety of sweet or savoury applications.

1. In a medium saucepan, gently heat the cream to 85°C (185°F). Add the lemon juice, stir to combine and continue to maintain the temperature of 85°C for 5 minutes until thickened.

2. Remove the pan from the heat and cool for 40 minutes.

3. Carefully strain into a fine-mesh sieve lined with muslin (cheesecloth), place over a bowl and leave to drain in the refrigerator overnight.

4. Transfer the mascarpone to a clean container.

RECIPE TYPE *base*

WOOD TYPE
stone fruit

HEAT
gentle embers

ADDITIONAL EQUIPMENT
sugar thermometer, muslin (cheesecloth)

INGREDIENTS
500 ml (17 fl oz/2 cups) Smoked cream (below)

1 tablespoon lemon juice

NOTES
The mascarpone needs to be refrigerated overnight, so begin this recipe a day ahead of time.

The smoked mascarpone will keep for up to 8 days in the refrigerator.

Smoked cream

MAKES 1 LITRE (34 FL OZ/4 CUPS)

Smoked cream is great for use as a base in many preparations, from butter to ice cream. The rich fat of cream makes it a great vehicle to carry the flavour of smoke, but it is best to choose a light fruit wood with a milder, sweeter profile for smoking. It is important that the two work together in harmony so that the flavour of the smoke doesn't overpower the natural taste of the cream.

1. Light a fire in a cool wood-fired oven using a small piece of fruit wood. Leave to burn down for 30 minutes to a small bed of glowing embers.

2. Pour 500 ml (17 fl oz/2 cups) of the cream into a shallow dish and place in the oven. Place a small piece of fruit wood on the embers, and quickly close the door. A thin blue smoke should emanate from the oven.

3. Allow the smoke to infuse the cream for 5 minutes.

4. Open the oven door and add the remaining cream, whisking to distribute evenly.

5. Repeat the smoking for a further 5 minutes. Taste the cream to ensure the desired balance of flavour between smoke and dairy has been achieved.

6. Pass the cream through a fine-mesh sieve and chill immediately. Store refrigerated for up to 5 days, using as required.

RECIPE TYPE *base*

WOOD TYPE
apple or plum

HEAT
indirect, gentle embers

ADDITIONAL EQUIPMENT
wood-fired oven

INGREDIENTS
1 litre (34 fl oz/4 cups) jersey (double/heavy) cream, minimum fat content of 45%

Smoked butter

MAKES 400 G (14 OZ)

In my years growing up in the UK and then training in a French kitchen, butter was one of the most important kitchen staples; it was incorporated into every dish and served with every meal. Yet in spite of over-beating cream on numerous occasions in the past, I had never made butter. It wasn't until I lived in Spain, where everything is cooked with olive oil, that I wanted to pursue it further. With cows, goats and sheep, the Basque country boasts a rich dairy industry, producing cheese, but not butter, so we decided to give it a go. But first we had to learn from the best, so we drove seven hours to a small farmstead just on the outskirts of Nantes in France. There we found an old housewife who milked her grass-fed cows for market, retaining the cream on the surface to make butter by hand. The naturally occurring lactic acid had matured and cultured the cream, resulting in a tangy richness. Sitting on a stool, she slowly worked the cream, her only equipment a traditional wooden bowl and her hand. We watched as she beat the thick cream with her hand until it gave way to rich curds and buttermilk. As she kneaded the paste, tears of buttermilk wept on the surface. I noticed the colour deepening, resulting in a rich, yellow butter.

Butter is a pure expression of the land, with a notable variation in taste in the spring, when the cows are in the fields feeding on succulent grasses, herbs and flowers. In the winter, they survive on leaner rations so the taste of winter butter, while still opulent, is markedly different.

Making good butter is a simple process but you do need to follow a particular sequence. Speed and delicate precision are required to ensure the best outcomes in terms of taste, texture and appearance.

1. Place the smoked cream into a large bowl and leave it for 36 hours to ripen in a cool place (6–8°C/45°F).

2. Using a whisk, beat to a stiff cream. Continue whisking the cream until it is just on the point of splitting. Remove the whisk and scrape down the sides with a spatula.

3. With a clean hand, continue to mix the cream; the temperature of your hand will help it to separate. You will notice the mixture loosening and splitting, with a texture resembling ricotta curds as the cream breaks into butterfat globules. A deep sunny yellow will develop and the buttermilk will separate from the butter.

4. Strain the buttermilk and reserve for later use (see pages 114, 124 and 201).

5. Knead the butter using your hands, squeezing to release the buttermilk. Place the butter in a container and cover with chilled filtered water, which will rinse it, cool it down and firm it slightly. This makes handling easier. Leave for 5 minutes before draining the water.

6. Repeat the rinsing with the water two more times until the water runs completely clear.

7. Gather the butter in your hands, squeeze out any excess water and place it in a clean mixing bowl. Season with salt to taste. The salt will draw out the remaining droplets of water, which will weep on the surface.

8. Wrap well in baking paper and chill until required. Enjoy as it is, or for a decadent seasonal treat, serve on top of grilled bread with shavings of black truffle.

RECIPE TYPE *base*

INGREDIENTS

1 litre (34 fl oz/4 cups) Smoked cream (page 225)

filtered water, chilled

fleur de sel or sea salt

NOTES

The smoked cream needs time to ripen, so begin the recipe at least 36 hours ahead of time.

Butter should be wrapped tightly, stored in a dark place and away from strong-tasting ingredients. This helps to prevent it becoming rancid or picking up undesirable odours. Butter is best served at 14°C (60°F).

006

Wheat

Bread

MAKES 1 × 800 G (1 LB 12 OZ) LOAF

I once took my 'mother' on holiday. I wanted to introduce her to a good friend in Queenstown, and I decided that the clean air and water of New Zealand might do her some good. Unfortunately, she didn't travel too well. In spite of clearing customs, she couldn't cope with the pressure on board the plane. She exploded, mainly taking her frustrations out on my luggage, which never fully recovered. It is just as well that I love my mother. Of course, the 'mother' is the naturally fermented yeasts that give life to bread. The combination of flour and water is basic but the result is a complex production of organic acids, alcohols and carbon dioxide that give bread its savoury tang and natural rise. I started my mother six years ago using a rye flour base and, as we were living on the Sunshine Coast of Queensland at the time, pineapple juice. The beauty of a mother is that it tells the story of a time and a place with yeasts, flour, air and water that are unique to its environment. Just like the best stories, it can be passed on to friends or family who can make it their own, adding further layers to the story before passing it on themselves.

There is nothing like making bread to make you appreciate the simple beauty of ingredients. Above all others, making bread is a magical process that sees flour and water ferment to transform into cloud-like heavenly bread. I love how the nutty richness of spelt combines with the caramel notes of the malt, and how cooking in a wood fire results in the most incredibly smoky and toothsome crust.

Mother

1. In a clean container, combine 100 ml (3½ fl oz) of the water and 100 g (3½ oz) of the flour.

2. Leave in a cool place for 3 days until the mixture shows signs of life, producing bubbles on the surface.

3. Combine 100 g (3½ oz) of the mother with 100 ml (3½ fl oz) of the water and 100 g (3½ oz) of the flour (this is known as feeding). Discard the remaining mother.

4. Leave for 1 day, then repeat the feeding. Feed the mother every 12 hours until it is strong enough to bake bread. To test this, place a spoon of the mother into a container of water. If it sinks, continue to feed the mother twice per day. When the mother holds together and floats, it is ready.

5. The mother will continue to develop over time, so be sure to retain 100 g (3½ oz) after each use for future baking. If you need more, simply increase the amount of flour and water when feeding.

RECIPE TYPE *savoury*

WOOD TYPE
stone fruit

HEAT
indirect, gentle embers

ADDITIONAL EQUIPMENT
large round proving basket, wood-fired or Dutch oven, laser thermometer, grill cooling rack

---

INGREDIENTS

**For the mother
(makes 300 g/10 ½ oz)**

600 ml (20½ fl oz) filtered water

600 g (1 lb 5 oz) strong wholemeal (whole-wheat) bread flour

For the bread

80 g (2¾ oz) Mother (see above)

280 ml (9½ fl oz) warm filtered water

250 g (9 oz) strong wholemeal (whole-wheat) bread flour

100 g (3½ oz) spelt flour

50 g (1¾ oz) malt flour

10 g (¼ oz) salt

20 g (¾ oz) rice flour, to dust

NOTES

Prepare the mother 6 days in advance. Unless you are planning to make bread daily, feed the mother once after use and store in a clean container in the refrigerator until required. When needed, remove from the refrigerator and feed twice prior to use until it is active and bubbling.

Prepare the bread 1 day in advance.

ALTERNATIVE METHOD

Bake in a Dutch oven over a fire, or in a conventional oven preheated to 250°C (480°F).

Bread

1. Combine the mother and 200 ml (7 fl oz) of warm water in a large bowl. Add the flours and, using your hands, combine to form a rough dough.

2. Rest for 15 minutes before kneading to form a smooth and silky dough. Cover and allow to rest for 30 minutes.

3. Add the salt and the remaining 80 ml (2½ fl oz/⅓ cup) of warm water, which will cause the dough to break apart a little. Continue working the mixture to bring it back together, forming a smooth dough.

4. Place the dough in a clean bowl, cover with a clean tea towel (dish towel) and leave to rest for 30 minutes.

5. Working in the bowl, wet your hands to stretch and fold the dough over itself, tucking the folds underneath. This will work to strengthen and develop the gluten in the flour. Leave to rest for 30 minutes.

6. Repeat the stretching and folding 3 times, rotating the dough at a 90 degree angle each time. Ensuring to rest the dough for 30 minutes each time.

7. Carefully turn the dough out onto a floured surface and gently shape and tuck the dough under to form a round. Generously dust the inside of the proving basket with rice flour. Put the dough into it, placing the smooth side down. Cover with a tea towel to prevent a skin forming on the top. Leave to prove for 1 hour until the dough has doubled in size, then place in the refrigerator for 12 hours.

8. Light your wood-fired oven (or prepare your embers if you are using a Dutch oven). Leave to burn until the fire dies down, resulting in gentle embers. You are aiming to bring the wood-fired oven to a temperature of 250°C (480°F) on the base.

9. Remove the dough from the refrigerator and leave for 3 hours to come up to room temperature.

10. Gently turn the dough out onto a piece of baking paper and, with a sharp knife, score the top of the loaf with even incisions.

11. Slide the bread into the wood-fired oven, closing the door immediately.

12. Bake for 20 minutes, after which time you should either open the door slightly or rake the embers to reduce the temperature slightly. Continue baking the bread for a further 30 minutes; the bread should have a deeply coloured crust. To test if the bread is ready, tap on its base - it should sound hollow. Carefully remove from the oven to cool on a grill cooling rack.

Black bread

MAKES 1 × 500 G (1 LB 2 OZ) LOAF

Last year I was invited to Tallinn to speak at Sauce, a conference uniting chefs and restaurants of the Baltic countries with those from around the world. It was my first time in Estonia but it reminded me of Australia, in that it has developed a cuisine adapted from other countries, in particular Germany, Sweden, Denmark and Russia. We were made welcome by humble generosity and simple food made with locally sourced ingredients. The stand-out for me was the deliciously dark and flavoursome bread known as *leib*, which plays an important role in Estonian culture. While there are many countries with a tradition of black bread, Estonian black bread is something truly unique, with secret recipes that vary from family to family. While the inclusion of rye produces a denser crumb, the combination of treacle, cocoa and coffee results in richly toasted, dark and flavoursome bread.

1. Combine the mother and the warm water in a large bowl. Add both flours and combine to form a rough dough. Cover and allow to rest for 30 minutes.

2. In a small pan, combine the seeds and toast over a medium heat for 4–5 minutes to release their essential oils.

3. In a small saucepan over a medium-low heat, combine the treacle, brown sugar, cocoa, coffee, salt and water. Stir constantly until just combined and the sugar is melted, then add the seeds. Allow to cool to room temperature.

4. Add the treacle mixture to the dough and combine. The treacle mixture will cause the dough to break apart a little, but continue working it to form a sticky dough.

5. Place the dough in a clean bowl, cover with a clean tea towel (dish towel) and leave to rise for 1 hour. Wet your hands and, working in the bowl, stretch and fold the dough over itself, tucking the folds underneath. (This will help to strengthen the gluten in the flour.) Leave the dough to rest for 30 minutes.

6. Carefully turn the dough out on to a floured surface, and gently shape and tuck the dough under to form a round.

7. Generously dust the inside of a large, round proving basket with rye flour. Put the dough into it, placing the smooth side down. Cover with a tea towel to prevent a skin forming on the top.

8. Leave to prove for 4 hours until the dough has doubled in size.

9. Light your wood-fired oven or, if using a Dutch oven, prepare your embers. Allow to burn until the fire dies down, resulting in gentle embers. You are aiming to bring the wood-fired oven to a temperature of 250°C (480°F) on the base.

10. Gently turn the bread out on to a floured baking tray and, with a sharp knife, score the top of the loaf with even incisions. Slide the bread into the oven, closing the door to the oven immediately.

11. Bake for 25 minutes, after which time you should either open the door slightly or rake the embers to reduce the temperature slightly. Continue baking the bread for a further 20 minutes. To test if the bread is done, tap it on its base - it should sound hollow. Carefully remove from the oven and allow to cool completely before slicing.

RECIPE TYPE *savoury*

WOOD TYPE
ironbark

HEAT
indirect, gentle embers

ADDITIONAL EQUIPMENT
*round proving basket,
wood-fired oven or Dutch oven
laser thermometer*

INGREDIENTS

100 g (3½ oz) Mother (page 232)

200 ml (7 fl oz) warm filtered water

100 g (3½ oz/1 cup) rye flour

350 g (12½ oz/2⅓ cups) wholemeal (whole-wheat) flour, plus extra for dusting

30 g (1 oz) linseeds (flax seeds)

60 g (2 oz/½ cup) sunflower seeds

1 teaspoon caraway seeds

1 teaspoon fennel seeds

20 g (¾ oz) treacle

15 g (½ oz) soft brown sugar

20 g (¾ oz) Dutch (unsweetened) cocoa powder

1 tablespoon coffee beans, finely ground

2 teaspoons salt

280 ml (9½ fl oz) filtered water

ALTERNATIVE METHOD

Bake the bread in a Dutch oven over a fire, or in a conventional oven preheated to 250°C (480°F).

Flatbread

trout roe, crème fraîche

MAKES 10

Flatbread was around long before the first oven, needing only a single hot surface on which to cook. The history of bread dates back to neolithic times, when lumps of dough were baked on hot stones placed in the embers of a wood fire. The high heat of the embers causes the bread to puff and toast while the slight blistering introduces a smoky note.

1. Prepare your embers and arrange a grill approximately 10 cm (4 in) above the embers.

2. In a large bowl, combine the flour and mother, kneading together to form a soft dough.

3. Cover and leave to rest for 20 minutes. Add the toasted fennel seeds, salt and warm water, which will cause the dough to break apart a little. Continue working to bring it back together into a dough.

4. Knead on a lightly floured surface for 10 minutes until silky and smooth.

5. Divide the dough into 10 balls each weighing 60 g (2 oz) and flatten slightly. On a floured surface, roll each ball out to a circumference of 15 cm (6 in).

6. Grill the flatbread on the grill for 2 minutes on each side, turning when it is puffed and toasted.

7. Transfer the flatbread to a tray and cover with a clean tea towel (dish towel). Repeat the process until all flatbreads have been grilled.

8. Combine the crème fraîche with the lime zest and juice. Season with salt to taste.

9. Serve the flatbreads with the crème fraîche dotted on top and finish with the trout roe, the rocket and the rocket flowers.

RECIPE TYPE *savoury*

WOOD TYPE
ironbark

HEAT
indirect, medium-intense embers

ADDITIONAL EQUIPMENT
grill

INGREDIENTS

300 g (10½ oz) unbleached wheat flour, plus extra for dusting

300 g (10½ oz) Mother (page 232)

½ teaspoon fennel seeds, toasted

½ teaspoon sea salt, plus extra to season

2 tablespoons warm filtered water

200 g (7 oz) crème fraîche

zest and juice of ½ lime

200 g (7 oz) ocean trout roe

½ bunch flowering rocket (arugula)

007

Bases

Chicken stock

MAKES 2 LITRES (68 FL OZ/8 CUPS)

1. Thoroughly wash the chicken carcasses and wings in cold water. Drain and add to a large heavy-based stockpot with the water.

2. Bring to the boil, skimming impurities as they rise to the surface.

3. Add the rest of the ingredients to the pot, reduce the heat and simmer for 2 hours, skimming occasionally.

4. Remove, drain through a fine-mesh sieve into a clean container. Allow to cool, then refrigerate for 6 hours, removing any fat from the surface when it sets. The stock can be kept for up to 3 days in the refrigerator or up to 2 months in the freezer.

INGREDIENTS

2 whole free-range chicken carcases

1 kg (2 lb 3 oz) free-range chicken wings

4 litres (135 fl oz/16 cups) filtered water

2 onions, peeled and quartered

4 carrots, peeled and halved

4 celery stalks, halved

4 garlic cloves, peeled

4 parsley stalks

Salt brine, 5%

MAKES 5 LITRES (169 FL OZ/20 CUPS)

Brining can be a great technique to apply to specific meats as the process of osmosis sees the meat absorb and retain juices even after it is cooked. The exposure to salt also helps to break down proteins, making the meat softer and juicier as a result. However, the process of brining must be adapted to suit the particular protein. If the concentration of salt is too high or the meat is left for too long in the brine, it can be unpalatable.

1. In a large, deep saucepan, combine the salt with 2 litres (68 fl oz/8 cups) of water.

2. Bring to the boil, stirring to dissolve the salt.

3. Remove the pan from the heat and pour in the remaining water. Allow to cool and refrigerate to chill completely before using for brining.

INGREDIENTS

250 g (9 oz) table sea salt (non-iodised)

5 litres (169 fl oz/20 cups) filtered water

Tomato water

MAKES 200 ML (7 FL OZ)

Made well and in season, this simple juice captures the lively essence of tomatoes with their unique balance of sweetness and acidity. Incorporating the tomato skins with the juice lends a fragrant golden hue, while fennel and celery provide a clean vegetal note. Its versatility means that, as well as making a good vegetable stock, it can lighten dressings and sauces, lend a fresh acidity to caramel and serve as a refreshing palate cleanser when chilled.

1. With a hand blender, blitz together the chopped tomatoes, fennel, celery and a pinch of salt.

2. Pass through a fine-mesh sieve lined with muslin (cheesecloth) set over a large bowl. Leave to sit for 1½ hours to drain. After this time, a sufficient amount of tomato water should have filtered through.

3. Transfer to a clean container and refrigerate until needed. It can be kept for up to 3 days.

ADDITIONAL EQUIPMENT
muslin (cheesecloth)

INGREDIENTS

500 g (1 lb 2 oz) cherry tomatoes, chopped

80 g (2¾ oz) fennel bulb, roughly chopped

¼ celery stalk, roughly chopped

pinch of sea salt

Smoked water

MAKES 1 LITRE (34 FL OZ/4 CUPS)

While it may seem a little odd, water can be smoked for use in cooking. It can give greater depth to a vegetable stock, lighten chocolate (see Banana ice cream, page 204) and even serve as a base in drinks. Ice gives the water a greater surface area for the smoke to act upon while making sure the water doesn't evaporate during the smoking process.

1. Light a fire in a cool wood-fired oven using a small piece of fruit wood. Leave to burn down for 30 minutes to a small bed of glowing embers.

2. Pour the water into a shallow dish and place in the oven. Place a small piece of fruit wood on the embers. Quickly close the door. A thin blue smoke should emanate from the oven. Allow the smoke to infuse the water for 4 minutes.

3. Remove the door and add the ice to the water in the dish. Repeat the smoking for a further 4 minutes.

4. Pass through a fine-mesh sieve and chill immediately.

WOOD TYPE
fruit wood

HEAT
indirect, gentle embers

ADDITIONAL EQUIPMENT
wood-fired oven

INGREDIENTS
500 ml (17 fl oz/2 cups) filtered water

500 g (1 lb 2 oz) ice made from filtered water

Smoked oil

MAKES 300 ML (10 FL OZ)

Like most fats, oil absorbs smoke readily and can be used as a vehicle for cooking (such as in the Egg cream, page 81) or incorporated in a dressing. However, it is important that the oil is not heated above 80°C (175°F) during smoking, as this impairs the delicate smokiness of the fruit wood.

1. Light a fire in a cool wood-fired oven using a small piece of fruit wood. Leave to burn down for 30 minutes to a small bed of glowing embers.

2. Pour the oil into a shallow dish and place in the oven. Place a small piece of fruit wood on the embers and quickly close the door. A thin blue smoke should emanate from the oven.

3. Allow the smoke to infuse the oil for 8 minutes. Remove and allow to cool.

4. Pass the oil through an oil filter and reserve until use.

WOOD TYPE
fruit wood, preferably apple, olive or orange

HEAT
indirect, gentle embers

ADDITIONAL EQUIPMENT
wood-fired oven, sugar thermometer, oil filter

INGREDIENTS
150 ml (5 fl oz) grapeseed oil

150 ml (5 fl oz) fruity, mild extra-virgin olive oil, such as arbequina or koroneiki

NOTE
The oil can be stored in a container in a cool, dark place for up to 2 months.

Fermented chilli paste

MAKES 500 G (1 LB 2 OZ)

Making fermented chilli paste is a great way to use the liquid from fermented cucumbers (page 114), the whey from homemade ricotta (page 224) and any chilli trimmings. The simple process of lactic fermentation results in a rich, complex paste with an amazing aroma and a fiery flavour. You can use whatever chillies you like, depending on how hot you can handle it.

1. Combine all the ingredients in a food processor to form a paste.

2. Pour into a sterilised jar and seal tightly. Leave to ferment, out of direct light, in a cool place for 5 days, by which time the paste should be gently bubbling with life.

3. Once fermented, refrigerate until needed.

INGREDIENTS

500 g (1 lb 2 oz) chilli peppers, stems removed and green caps retained (see Note)

2 garlic cloves, peeled and minced

1 tablespoon sugar

½ teaspoon sea salt

25 ml (¾ fl oz) whey or liquid from the fermented cucumbers (page 114)

NOTES

Like tomatoes, chilli peppers have a lot of flavour in their green tops or calyx, so these are best kept on the fruit when fermenting.

The fermented chilli paste can be kept in the refrigerator for up to 6 months.

Smoked kombucha

MAKES 2 LITRES (68 FL OZ/8 CUPS)

While most people regard kombucha as a relatively new drink, it has been produced for 2000 years. Originating in China, kombucha is a sweetened tea that is fermented by a symbiotic colony of bacteria and yeast (SCOBY – a 'mother' by another name). Healthy SCOBY and the best-quality tea are the foundations to producing a well-flavoured kombucha. Once made, kombucha can be kept for a few months as long as it is refrigerated. As well as being a refreshing beverage that pairs well with food (particularly when it comes to fatty or spicy foods), it has many purported health benefits including aiding digestion. It can also be used in many dishes, such as the pink lady apples that accompany the pork on page 187.

1. In a medium saucepan, bring the water, smoked water and sugar to a simmer, stirring until the sugar has dissolved.

2. Remove from the heat and add the green and black teas. Leave to steep for 4 minutes, before passing through a fine-mesh sieve into a large sterilised jar. Allow to cool (see Note).

3. Once cool, add the SCOBY before placing a breathable seal over the jar, such as a square of muslin (cheesecloth) fastened with an elastic band.

4. Store in a cool place out of direct sunlight for 12 days to ferment, after which time the kombucha should have developed acidity, resulting in a tangy fragrance.

5. Using a slotted spoon, remove the SCOBY. Pour the liquid into a sterilised bottle and refrigerate until needed.

ADDITIONAL EQUIPMENT

muslin (cheesecloth)

INGREDIENTS

1 litre (34 fl oz/4 cups) filtered water

750 ml (25½ fl oz/3 cups) Smoked water (page 241)

250 g (9 oz) sugar

2 tablespoons green tea leaves

2 tablespoons black tea leaves

2 tablespoons SCOBY (see Note)

NOTE

It is important that the liquid is cool before introducing the SCOBY. Like the Mother (page 232) the SCOBY is alive and must be maintained. This is best done by continuing to make more kombucha. You can also combine the SCOBY with alcohol (wine or spirit) for 3 months if you want to produce vinegar.
You can buy SCOBY online or from health-food shops.

The kombucha can be kept in the refrigerator for up to 8 months.

Ginger syrup

MAKES 200 ML (7 FL OZ)

1. Prepare your embers, which should be slow burning.

2. Place the sliced ginger on a grill cooling rack approximately 10 cm (4 in) above the embers and grill gently until light golden and slightly smoky.

3. Remove the ginger and place it in a small saucepan with the water, agave nectar and lime zest. Bring to the boil and simmer for 5 minutes. Allow to cool and infuse for 1 hour.

4. Transfer to a food processor and blend for 30 seconds before passing through a fine-mesh sieve into a sterilised jar. Refrigerate until needed.

WOOD TYPE
fruit wood

HEAT
gentle embers

ADDITIONAL EQUIPMENT
grill cooling rack

INGREDIENTS

30 g (1 oz) ginger, thinly sliced lengthways

100 ml (3½ fl oz) filtered water

100 ml (3½ fl oz) agave nectar

zest of 1 lime

NOTE

The ginger syrup can be kept in the refrigerator for up to 8 months.

Elderflower cordial

MAKES 2 LITRES (68 FL OZ/8 CUPS)

The creamy white flowers of elder burst into blossom for just a few weeks in summer, bearing a heady and heavenly fragrance. Historically, elder (*Sambucus nigra*) was viewed as a sacred tree and it is thought that the name, elder, comes from the Anglo-Saxon word *æld*, meaning fire, because the hollow stems were once used as bellows to feed air into the fire. The tree has many uses. The green berries can be pickled like capers, or left until autumn (fall) to ripen to the deep purple clusters that lend a tart kick to any dish, while the flowers can be made into fritters or the floral cordial below. Dilute as required for a refreshing drink or incorporate into a dessert, such as the pavlova on page 211.

1. Gently heat the sugar with the water, lemon zest and juice in a saucepan, stirring until the sugar has dissolved.

2. Bring the mixture to the boil and remove from the heat.

3. Immediately add the elderflowers face down, ensuring that they are submerged in the syrup.

4. Add the citric acid, cover and leave to steep for 24 hours.

5. Pass the cordial through a fine-mesh sieve lined with muslin (cheesecloth) into a sterilised jar or bottle. Refrigerate until needed.

INGREDIENTS

1 kg (2 lb 3 oz) sugar

1 litre (34 fl oz/4 cups) filtered water

zest and juice of 1 lemon

100 g (3½ oz) fresh elderflowers (see Note)

40 g (1½ oz) citric acid

ADDITIONAL EQUIPMENT
muslin (cheesecloth)

NOTES

The flowers contain all the fragrance and are delicate, so be sure to handle carefully, picking through to remove bugs rather than washing vigorously.

The cordial needs time to steep, so begin this recipe a day ahead of time.

It can be kept in the refrigerator for up to 8 months.

Salsa verde

MAKES 250 G (9 OZ)

This vibrant green sauce boasts countless variations and manages to transverse many places including Italy, Spain, France and South America (where it is known as *chimichurri*). Its grassy, peppery nature is enriched with anchovies and it is delicious with everything from vegetables to grilled fish (see Salt-crusted snapper, page 158) as well as red meat, such as lamb and beef.

1. Combine the herbs in a blender along with the garlic and ice cube. Blend on medium speed, stopping at intervals to ensure the herbs are evenly processed.

2. Add the capers, mustard, vinegar and anchovy fillets and blend on medium-high speed until combined. Be careful not to overwork the mixture or it will discolour.

3. With the machine running on medium speed, gradually add the olive oil in a slow and steady stream, scraping down the sides with a spatula. Turn the machine to high and process for 10 seconds.

4. Check the seasoning and consistency, then transfer to an airtight jar. Pour a thin layer of olive oil on top of the salsa verde to prevent oxidisation. Store in the refrigerator where it will keep for 2 days.

INGREDIENTS

1 bunch flat-leaf (Italian) parsley, leaves picked, washed and dried

½ bunch basil, leaves picked, washed and dried

½ bunch mint, leaves picked, washed and dried

1 garlic clove

1 large ice cube

30 g (1 oz) capers in brine, drained and rinsed

1 tablespoon Dijon mustard

1 tablespoon red-wine vinegar

3 anchovy fillets

250 ml (8½ fl oz/1 cup) extra-virgin olive oil, such as arbequina, plus extra for covering

sea salt

Pil-pil sauce

Pil-pil sauce is one of the staples of Basque cuisine, in which the gelatine from the grilling juices, olive oil and vinegar is agitated to form a rich emulsion. Traditionally it is made by gently heating white gelatinous fish such as cod or hake in olive oil, garlic and chilli until the gelatine of the fish is released, resulting in a rich, fatty sauce. While particularly effective with fish, the technique can be applied to a variety of ingredients straight from the grill, where the natural juices are combined with oil and acidity to form a natural dressing. This is a technique used often throughout this book. Choose oil and an acid that will complement the ingredients. Using a fine-mesh sieve as a whisk helps to incorporate air and emulsify the sauce.

1. In a small saucepan, gently warm the oil, then pour it over the grilling juices or stock. Add the vinegar or citrus juice for acidity, then strain all the juices and the oil back into the pan. Return to a low heat.

2. Strain through a fine-mesh sieve while agitating the sieve continuously until an emulsion is formed.

3. Taste and adjust seasoning and consistency. Serve immediately.

INGREDIENTS

3 parts oil, such as olive, grapeseed or nut oil

2 parts grilling juices (on the tray following grilling) or stock

1 part vinegar or citrus juice

sea salt

Glossary

AGRETTI The Italian word for a green succulent found in coastal regions – the leaves (*salsola soda*) are edible.

À LA FICELLE Literally hanging 'by a string' – a side or cut of meat or a whole bird hanging from string and cooking over fire.

ASADOR Is the Spanish word for a fire on which one can cook animals on a spit, cross or by hanging using other means. It also refers to a Spanish grill restaurant.

BANKSIA Australian native plant with bottlebrush flowers and leathery leaves. It is well-adapted to survive Australian bushfires; in reaction to fire, the plant's woody fruits open, dispersing the seeds to generate new growth.

BARILLA Also known as Coorong spinach, and related to warrigal greens, it is found in the first line of vegetation on beaches around south eastern Australia. It has a delicate flavour and a thick, small leaf covered in water storage cells.

BEACH HERBS Native greens, including barilla, karkalla, samphire, seablite and warrigal greens (to name a few), growing where the land meets the sea.

BINCHOTAN Also called white charcoal, *binchotan* is high-quality Japanese charcoal that produces extremely high heat and conversely cools quite rapidly.

BOTTARGA Salted and dried mullet roe.

BRAINSPIKING The fastest and most humane method of killing seafood. A sharp spike or the point of a knife is inserted directly into the hindbrain. It is best carried out when the fish is in a relaxed state; this is aided by chilling the fish.

CARAPACE The large, hard upper shell of a crustacean that helps to protect the body and eyes from predators.

CHURRASCO A South American word for meat cooked on skewers over fire.

DULSE A red seaweed or algae that grows wild on the northern coasts of the Atlantic and Pacific oceans. It is usually sold dried.

ELVER A young eel.

FINGER LIME A native Australian microcitrus with a smooth, slender and elongated shape. Available in many colours.

FLEUR DE SEL Meaning 'flower of salt' in French, it is a salt that forms as a thin, delicate crust on the surface of seawater as it evaporates.

FOIE GRAS The liver of a fattened goose or duck.

IKE-JIME A Japanese term meaning 'live killing'. It is a method of brainspiking seafood to ensure immediate brain death. It is the fastest and most humane way to kill seafood and results in a superior eating experience.

KARKALLA A round-leafed succulent found near the surf throughout southern Australia.

LACTONES Internally formed esters of hydroxycarboxylic acids, which can occur in essential oils and have a high flavour value.

OGATAN Japanese charcoal briquette made from compressed sawdust.

PACHAMANCA A traditional Peruvian dish used to slow cook food with the aid of fire and/or hot stones.

PARILLA The South American word for grill, or cooking over fire.

PINTXOS The word used to describe small snacks in Spain, especially in the Basque region.

SALAMANDER A grill characterised by heat coming from overhead. It takes its name from the salamander, a mythical amphibian believed to be immune to fire.

SALTBUSH A large, robust Australian native bush that produces leaves that are often described as a 'salty herb'.

SAMPHIRE A native succulent, also referred to as sea asparagus. Its name is derived from the French word for Saint Peter (Saint Pierre), the patron saint of fishermen. In England it is also referred to as glasswort, as marsh samphire ashes were once used to fabricate glass.

SEABLITE A small, fern-like coastal succulent related to samphire that grows in estuaries and mudflats.

WAKAME An edible seaweed or sea vegetable.

WARRIGAL GREENS A leafy spinach-like native that is rich in vitamin C and grows wild along Australia's coast. The word 'warrigal' refers to its 'wild' cultivation, but it is sometimes called Botany Bay spinach or Cook's cabbage, as the Indigenous Australian people gave it to Captain Cook's crew to help cure them of scurvy.

Index

Acknowledgements

This book would not have been possible without a great deal of help, guidance and support from a lot of people.

Firstly, thank you to my publisher, Jane Willson, for believing in this book and for the freedom and tolerance she gave me in writing it. To Loran McDougall, Kate Wanwimolruk and the Hardie Grant team for their guidance and patience throughout the whole process. Writing a book is almost as hard as opening a restaurant.

For making this cookbook with me, my sincere thanks must go to Elizabeth Hewson for her unwavering understanding and encouragement together with her amazing organisation and ability to crack the whip when necessary … everybody needs a Lizzie in their lives.

Thank you to all the people who made the book come to life. Nikki To (AC) for her incredible photography and for capturing fire in its element, and to Deb Kaloper, who is possibly the most well-equipped stylist I have ever met. To Anthony Huckstep for stringing together my stories, and to Murray Batten for his design under the guidance of Mark Campbell.

A special thank you to John Fink and Estelle Hoen for their support and for cooking up possibly the best paella during the shoot. To Nathan Cattell from Killalea National Park for allowing us to light up his beach, and to Paul and Susie Hewson for the use of their beautiful farm, which provided the backdrop for many of our shots.

To all the amazing suppliers and producers who I proudly work with on a daily basis, thank you all for your energy and support of this book. Paul Ashman and Nathan Chetcuti from Wood Trailer Functions, Justyn McGrigor from Murdoch Produce, Anthony Puharich and Andrew Kunze from Vic's Premium Quality Meats for continuing to work with me to create Australia's most amazing steak, Andrew Boyd from Martins Seafoods, Sally Gosper and Amber Hoult from Simon Johnson, Shady and Rose Wasef from Pioik Bakery, Gayle and Mike Quarmby from Outback Pride, Mike and Christa McDonald from Blackheath Firewood, Tim and Liz Johnstone from Johnstone Kitchen Gardens, Emmanuel Simitzis from Australian Live Seafood, David Cockerill from Cudgegong Valley Olives and Malcolm Greenwood for his beautiful ceramics, many of which incorporate the ashes from the fire.

Thank you to John Dixon and David Wynne from the NSW Teachers Federation for their support of Firedoor and for accommodating part of the shoot. To my Fink Group Family, in particular my business partner, Leon Fink, and chefs Peter Gilmore, Rob Kabboord and Ross Lusted.

To my entire Firedoor family, you are all the most amazing team of passionate individuals and I am proud to work with you. My thanks in particular to Raurri Fagan, Peter Raymond and Toby Robinson for their support and help in compiling and shooting the recipes.

To my gorgeous wife, Diana, for her infinite patience, her love, and the amazing job in bringing up our beautiful son, Alex – may he take more after his mother than his father. My grandmother, with whom I first cooked, I owe my passion and love for cooking to you. Thank you to my wonderful parents for a lifetime of love and support

And finally, thank you to Bittor Arguinzoniz for showing me the real beauty of fire … *eskerrik asko*.

References

My approach to cooking with fire has been shaped
through experience and by drawing on the knowledge and
observation of many people and cultures who cook with
fire. The information in this book is the sum of my practical
knowledge and the information I have gained and gathered
over the last ten years. The following are some sources that I
have referred to in compiling this book:

FRANCIS MALLMANN. *Seven Fires: Grilling the Argentine Way.*
Artisan: New York, 2009.

PAULA MARCOUX. *Cooking with Fire: From Roasting on a Spit
to Baking in a Tannur, Rediscovered Techniques and Recipes that
Capture the Flavors of Wood-fired Cooking.* Storey Publishing:
Massachusetts, 2014.

RICHARD WRANGHAM. *Catching Fire: How Cooking Made
Us Human.* Basic Books: New York, 2009.

CHRISTIAN F PUGLISI. *Relæ: A Book of Ideas.* Ten Speed
Press: New York, 2014.